Other books by Lauren Marie Filarsky . . .

The Star Horses Series

Emma and Starfire
The First Seahorse

Breaking Expectations

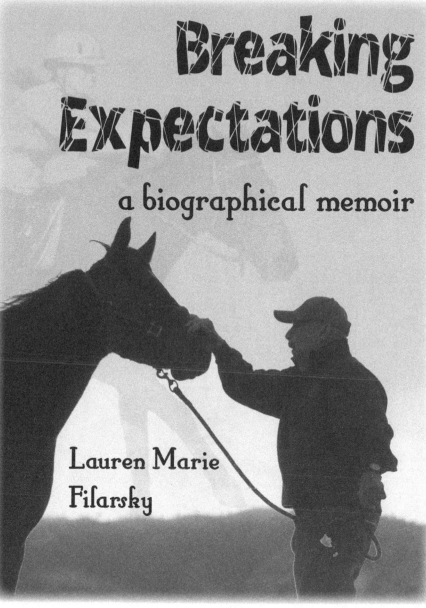

Breaking Expectations

a biographical memoir

Lauren Marie Filarsky

BInk

Bink Books

Bedazzled Ink Publishing Company • Fairfield, California

978-1-949290-37-0 paperback

Cover Photo
by
Jan Lundberg Photography

Cover Design
by

Bink Books
a division of
Bedazzled Ink Publishing, LLC
Fairfield, California
http://www.bedazzledink.com

For Dad and Steve Irwin.
Without you, none of this would have been possible.

"I know what it is to be in need, and I know what it is to have plenty. I have learned the secret of being content in any and every situation, whether well fed or hungry, whether living in plenty or in want. I can do everything through him who gives me strength."

— Philippians 4:12-13 (NIV)

Contents

Prologue
Roy's Gift

"BULLYING IS NO good," Roy stated with conviction, as a classroom full of fourth graders stared at him in rapt attention. "Other kids can be mean. They make fun of you for anything that is different. They call you names and make you feel bad about yourself. And that's no good. They tell you things that aren't true, but it still hurts." As he continued to speak, several children stared at the ground, unable to meet the empathetic brown eyes of the stooped man in front of them. Yet as I watched, they glanced up, powerless to resist, hopeful that Roy had the answer to heal their pain.

"When I was younger, people bullied me. They called me a retard and laughed at me. And it hurt. There was nothing I could do to fight back; I just had to walk away and try to ignore them."

Roy paused, and in the silence a little hand was lifted in the air.

"Yes?" he asked.

"Did you cry?" a voice whispered, too quiet for his aging ears to catch.

"What did you say?"

The girl took a deep breath. In the classroom of children still years away from their growth spurts, she was by far the smallest, nearly a head shorter than all her peers. Visibly working up her courage, she spoke louder. "When they bullied you, did you cry?"

"Yes." The single word hung in the air, echoing in the absolute silence of the classroom.

"Oh," she said, her eyes falling back to her desk. And then, unable to look away for long, she met Roy's understanding eyes and confessed in a rush. "I'm being bullied."

Without a moment's hesitation Roy walked to her side, his knees creaking as he knelt to embrace the tiny girl. I saw tears flow down her face as she hugged him fiercely back.

"I know, I know," he murmured to her, so quiet that only her closest neighbors could overhear. "You're going to be all right. No matter what they say to you, don't believe it. You are a wonderful person, and you are going to have a wonderful life. Just remember: I love you."

When the girl's tears finally stopped, Roy heaved himself back to his feet, using the desk for support. Across the classroom, another hand rose in the air.

"I get bullied too," came another small voice.

I watched in amazement as Roy continued to make his way around the room, hugging and encouraging the injured students who poured out their hardships to him, opening up their hearts in spite of the fact that less than an hour before he had been a total stranger to them. By the time he was finished, there was hardly a dry eye left in the classroom. But the weight of anguish had been lifted from many small shoulders, and instead peaceful smiles adorned their faces.

The bell rang, signaling the start of lunch hour, and as the students filed out the door they gave Roy one last hug and implored him to come back to their class.

"I'll try, but even if I don't you are all going to be all right," Roy promised.

Chapter 1
Small Town Celebrity

THEY SAY THAT in a small town everybody knows everyone else. In my hometown of 6,000 souls, there are a few too many people for that saying to be true. After a thousand or so, one face blurs into the next. But in the rural California farming community of Winters, there is a kernel of truth in that saying: Everyone knows Roy.

Roy doesn't have a driver's license, so he walks everywhere he needs to go. As he slowly shuffles down the sidewalks, his kind brown eyes are often crinkled in a smile as he greets passers-by: old friends, acquaintances, and the rare stranger. It's difficult to overlook Roy, but not because he stands out in any particular fashion due to looks or clothes. Roy is a short, thick-necked gentleman who usually wears a t-shirt and baggy jeans, which are held up by both a belt and suspenders. He has a shiny crown ringed by close-cropped stubble, although his bare pate is usually covered by a baseball cap featuring the logo of various local companies.

What catches your eye about Roy is his welcoming personality. While most people try to avoid eye contact with strangers, Roy makes an effort to greet people around him, whether pedestrians on the street or patrons at his favorite coffee shop.

My mom first caught a glimpse of Roy after my family moved to Winters in 1995, shortly after I began kindergarten. That year, Roy was the Honorary Grand Marshall of the town's annual spring celebration, the Youth Day Parade. There wasn't much to make him stand out from the rest of the parade entrants. He rode in the back of a convertible green Mustang and sported a brown suit in imitation of President Eisenhower, whom Roy had seen during a whistle-stop campaign when Roy was a boy. What made Roy stand out was the reaction of the spectators.

Most parade participants received scattered ovations from the crowd watching from the sidewalk, with larger rounds of applause and cheering reserved for acts of showmanship—the wailing siren of a firetruck or a majorette performing a difficult baton twirl. But when Roy passed, everyone noticed. Whistles, applause, and calls of "Hi, Roy!" and "Hey, it's Roy!" followed him down the streets. Roy beamed and waved at everyone, who cheered in the fashion usually reserved for rock stars and Hollywood celebrities.

So what is it that makes this man so remarkable and well-known? At first glance, it would seem that his whole life is the reflection of the Golden Rule; Roy loves people, and they in return love Roy. Everywhere he goes, Roy greets his friends with a hug and asks about them, their families, and their jobs. It's difficult to look him in the eye and mechanically respond, "I'm fine; how are you?" If something is wrong, Roy can see it, and he will immediately take your hand, squeeze it firmly, and ask, "You doing all right?"

One might think that this genuine love comes from a nurtured childhood and having close friends when he was growing up. In reality, Roy's youth was just the opposite.

Roy Ralph Irwin was born on July 6, 1938, in New York City. From the start, it was apparent that something was wrong. His umbilical cord was tangled at birth, and the shortage of oxygen caused irreparable damage. The doctors, his parents, and society at large immediately labeled him a "retard" and assumed that he wouldn't be able to do anything but menial labor throughout his life. Those expectations held true—for a while.

Roy's parents, Roy Frank Irwin and Glenys Helm Irwin, moved to a Detroit suburb when Roy was one year old, and he spent his early years in public school in the Detroit area. In the classroom, teachers wrote him off as a failure and didn't bother to teach him the basic skill that most Americans take for granted: literacy. On the playground, children laughed and ridiculed him, ganging up to tease "the retarded kid." When it came time to pick teams for a game of baseball one afternoon, neither team captain wanted Roy. Instead, Roy retreated to a nearby curb and cried while the players ignored him and enjoyed the game.

A nearby teacher noticed Roy sitting alone on the curb. The teacher asked Roy why he wasn't playing with the other children, and Roy tearfully told him the truth.

Upon hearing that Roy had been excluded from the game, the teacher brought Roy onto the field, gave him a bat, and lobbed a few pitches at him while the other boys looked on. Roy swung the bat, grazing the ball as it flew past him.

"Just keep your eyes on the ball, Roy," the teacher encouraged. "You'll get it."

And on the next pitch, Roy connected solidly, sending the ball sailing over the fence for the only home run of the game.

But the vindication of hitting a home run was not enough to help Roy succeed, either socially or academically. After watching their son struggle through childhood and feeling powerless to help improve his situation, Roy's parents followed the advice of Roy's uncle, who was a psychologist, and decided to get professional help for Roy. That help came in the form of Lapeer State Home and Training School, originally named The Michigan Home for the Feeble-Minded and Epileptic, which Roy began attending when he was twelve years old. While his parents thought that sending Roy to live at the institution would be for his benefit, it couldn't have been further from that. In the four years Roy attended the institution, the only things he learned were how to be a janitor and how to take abuse.

Roy says simply, "It was a hellhole. I don't know how I survived."

It wasn't any easier for Roy to make friends at the institution than it had been at the public school. Like Roy, the other residents had borne the brunt of scathing ridicule from children who should have been their peers, and they often expressed their pain in the only way they knew possible, by lashing out at each other. Roy's gentle nature made him just as much of a target as he had been in the public school system.

From the outside, the institution belied the inner turmoil: four hundred acres of picturesque green lawns were bisected by a gently flowing stream bordered by precisely placed, manicured trees. The buildings were tall, stately red-brick edifices, with slate-gray roofs and eye-catching white trim. Inside the dormitories, orderly rows of neatly made beds marched down the sides of long rooms, giving the impression of a hospital or orphanage. At night, quiet sobs echoed through the darkness. In the mornings, the booming gong of a bell signaled the start of the day, and if the residents didn't rise quickly enough, the beds were tipped over to dump their sleeping occupants on the cold, hard floor.

Roy learned how to clean by scrubbing the floors of the institution, kneeling with a bucket of hot, soapy water on the hard tiles, his shoes removed to keep them from getting soaked or tracking dirt. His back and neck muscles ached from the strain of hunching over, while his knees bruised on the unforgiving floor. One day while he was working, another student picked up one of the buckets of steaming water and threw it on Roy's bare feet, laughing as Roy yelled in pain from his burned skin.

Roy received no comfort or help from the adults in charge at the institution either. One afternoon when Roy was working, he went upstairs to ask the supervisor a question. He knocked on the thick oak door.

"Enter," came a clear, clipped voice from the other side.

Roy walked into the office. "Ex . . . ex . . . excuse me, s-s-s-sir." He had trouble pronouncing words, and would often delay mid-sentence as he struggled to recall the correct word. "I . . . I . . . I just . . . wanted . . . wanted to ask. . . ." He didn't get a chance to finish.

Apparently frustrated with Roy's stuttering and unwilling to waste his own precious time, the supervisor rose from his chair, grabbed Roy by his hair, and slammed his head twice against the solid oak door before throwing him out of the office.

"I'm busy," he snarled. "Don't bother me."

During Roy's first Christmas break from Lapeer, he took the train home to visit his parents. As he climbed into the passenger car, clutching his suitcase in one hand and his ticket in the other, the conductor stopped him.

"Where do you think you are going?" the conductor asked.

"H-h-home," Roy said, showing him the ticket.

The conductor looked Roy up and down; from his stuttering speech, he correctly guessed that Roy lived at the nearby institution. The residents of the institution were confined to the grounds and kept mostly out of sight of the rest of society; the conductor decided that nobody would want to be seated with a "feeble-minded" boy.

"Follow me," the conductor ordered. He led Roy outside and down the platform to where mail was being loaded into a boxcar. "You can ride in here."

Roy obediently clambered into the car and placed his suitcase on the floor to serve as a seat. For the two-hour train ride, he sat alone in the unheated train car, shivering and crying as the snow whipped past the train. The rhythmic clickety-clack of the wheels rolling down the track was only broken when the squealing brakes brought the train to a stop and the doors were opened so baggage and mail could be unloaded, allowing icy winds to swirl into the car and through his clothes.

When Roy finally reached his stop, he was lost.

"Follow the crowd," his dad had told him over the phone while Roy was at Lapeer. "They'll lead you the right way."

But the crowd scattered across the platform, passengers milling in every direction as they disembarked and moved toward different platforms to board other trains. There was no general flow of humanity for Roy to follow, and if there was a sign for the exit, Roy couldn't read it. Finally, he managed to make his way through the station, and the frightened, lonely child sat on his suitcase to wait for his dad to pick him up.

ROY'S PARENTS REALIZED how difficult Lapeer was for him, but with no other options available to them, they hoped that he would still be able to receive some benefits from attending the institution. The separation from her son was especially hard on Glenys, who had always tried to protect Roy, even when it was to his detriment. Glenys tried to shelter Roy from the hardships he faced in the world, but by doing so she sometimes prevented him from learning the skills necessary to be an independent adult. If Roy didn't know how to do something and asked for help, Glenys would simply take over and do it for him, rather than teaching him how to do it himself. It was a short-term solution that made life easier and Roy temporarily happy, but it laid the foundation of an unnecessary dependence on others that Roy would wrestle with his entire life.

Glenys unintentionally incapacitated Roy by teaching him to avoid adversity by ignoring and evading problems, rather than figuring out how to solve them. This wasn't just limited to learning new skills; Roy's father was a stern man, and he was often frustrated with the challenges of raising a child with a learning disability. But where Glenys was overprotective, Roy Senior reacted with harshness. He never raised a hand against his son, but neither did he praise or express love to him. Like most children, at the dinner table young Roy would chew with his mouth open, making loud noises with his lips.

"Quit smacking your lips!" his dad would snarl, the overreaction scaring Roy and causing him to shut down and stop eating. To make matters worse, Glenys would then hustle her son into the kitchen, where Roy could eat out of sight of his father and smack his lips all he wanted.

Loving Glenys despaired over her separation from her son, knowing that he was miserable at Lapeer, and she eventually insisted that Roy return home. On September 19, 1955, at the age of seventeen, Roy was discharged from the institution, which at the time had reached its peak patient population of 4,600. Roy was still unable to read or do basic math, but he managed to get jobs mowing lawns and working for the local school board.

Roy discovered what would become a lifelong passion for horses when he obtained a position as a stable boy at the Grosse Pointe Hunt Club, a riding stable whose membership ranks contained the names of many of Detroit's wealthy upper class, such as the Ford family. The stable and riding manager at the club, Clarence "Red" La Pearl, met Roy when he was building a parking lot for the school board. Red talked to Roy over a can of pop and saw a glimpse of Roy's potential. Afterward, Red used his influence to help Roy acquire a job at the ritzy club.

Roy mucked stalls and swept floors, working diligently to care for the horses under his charge. He knew next to nothing about the animals, other than that they were several times his size and potentially dangerous at both ends, with strong teeth and steel-shod hooves. But as he spent hours among them—bringing them hay, cleaning up their manure, and grooming them—he found something he wasn't expecting: peaceful companionship. The gentle giants responded to a quiet word, even if it was spoken with a stutter, and they reveled in the attention of getting petted and scratched; it didn't matter to them that Roy was different.

Roy started occasionally bringing his equine charges a special treat: a large gunnysack full of massive carrots, which he happily doled out to all the horses. Roy began to feel acceptance at the stables—the horses knew him, and even when he had no treats, they whinnied in greeting when they saw their friend and caretaker.

The horses weren't the only beings at the Grosse Pointe Hunt Club that accepted Roy for who he was. Many of the club members came to know and value the steadfast worker who cared for their horses. One of Roy's closest friends there was Jack Kirlin, who enjoyed talking with Roy during Roy's break from cleaning stalls. Their friendship endured long past Roy's time at the Hunt Club, and when he returned to visit Michigan decades later, Roy stayed in the home of Kirlin's daughter and son-in-law.

After a couple years of reliable work as a stable hand, Roy was promoted to night watchman. It was the first time Roy was ever given a position of responsibility, and he thrived in the trust bestowed upon him. Every night at eight o'clock, Dorothy Turri, the business manager who oversaw the clubhouse, started a fire in the guardroom furnace to keep Roy warm during his long, lonely vigil. He patrolled the grounds of the Hunt Club, armed with a trusty flashlight, watching over the multi-thousand dollar horses and keeping a lookout for vandals, thieves, and intruders meaning them harm.

One night, Roy heard a group of teenagers enter the stable. Whether they were merely looking for a place to party or they were maliciously intending to damage the property or scare the animals, Roy didn't know. But he did know that he wasn't going to let them near his beloved charges.

"Let's go get them, men!" Roy yelled, making a lot of noise as he ran toward the boys. The teens, who probably thought they were being chased by a group of watchmen rather than the solo guardian, scattered and fled the Hunt Club grounds.

Every morning after work, Roy was picked up by his dad or by his "baby" brother, Steve, who was fourteen years Roy's junior and just beginning to drive. Roy worked six nights a week, clocking in over sixty hours. The hours may have been long, but the pride and enjoyment he received from the trust placed in him were well worth it. He had found love from people outside of his family, and for the first time in his life, he was respected.

After Roy had worked four years at the Hunt Club, the Irwin family moved to Winters, California, leaving behind the frigid winters that were increasingly difficult on Glenys, who was becoming severely arthritic. Roy didn't want to leave, but as he hadn't been taught the necessary skills to live independently, he mournfully said goodbye to the horses he loved. Once the Irwins settled in California, Steve attended Winters High School while Roy worked different jobs in town, from apricot picker to school janitor.

Roy was at loss in the apricot orchards, despite working alongside his brother during Steve's summer vacation. A pair of "gringos" in a crowd of Mexican field workers, Roy and Steve stood out for more than the color of their skin or their natal language. The other workers had years of experience and filled their fruit baskets quickly, while Roy slowly plodded along and gradually filled his own tub, his brother at his side. But instead of scorning Roy, the other workers helped him learn to pick faster and taught him a few words and phrases in Spanish.

Despite the encouragement of the other workers, Roy and Steve didn't last too long in the apricot orchards. One afternoon, as Roy was picking fruit from the upper branches of a tree, his ladder slipped out from beneath him. Roy managed to grab ahold of a branch as the ladder crashed to the ground, clutching the ominously creaking limb and calling for help. Steve raced to his brother's aid, righted the ladder, and held it steady as Roy made his way back to the safety of the ground.

"Let's get out of here," Roy told Steve once his feet were firmly planted back on solid ground. "I'm not going to climb the trees like a monkey."

But Roy ran into a different kind of trouble at his next job. When he began working at the high school as a janitor, the man who supervised him treated Roy worse than an animal; he acted as if Roy couldn't understand anything and was unable to have any feelings.

"Look what I have to deal with," the man loudly told others within Roy's hearing.

Roy took the verbal abuse in silence, but it fueled his bitterness and anger.

The contrast of the janitor's contempt compared to the respect Roy had received at the Hunt Club was too much for Roy to handle. He drowned his despair at the local bars every night. Full of a riot of emotions that he couldn't control, Roy danced with pretty girls, "bent the elbow" with shots of hard liquor, and fought with anyone who dared ridicule him or call him a retard. Before long, his drinking habit spiraled into full-fledged alcoholism.

In 1978, when Roy was forty, his father died at the age of seventy-five. Steve was twenty-six, and he had moved out of the family house when he began college several years before, which left Roy and their mother alone together. But as Glenys's rheumatoid arthritis progressed, she became incapable of taking care of herself and her embittered son. In 1985, Steve was forced to leave his home in San Francisco and his job as a Greyhound bus driver in order to take care of his crippled mother and alcoholic brother.

From the moment Steve stepped across the threshold, he and Roy were at odds. No longer was Roy the benevolent older brother who would take Steve for rides in the basket of his bicycle. Instead, Roy was an angry and wounded adult who was unable to heal from his past trauma.

Steve, on the other hand, was no longer a child, despite the fact that Roy still called him his "baby brother." Rather, he was an independent young man who had to give up the pursuit of his dreams in order to care for two disabled family members—one physically, the other emotionally.

Things between Roy and Steve came to a head in 1988.

"I'm going to stop drinking this week," Roy told Steve, who didn't respond.

On Friday, Roy hit the bars again. The following Monday morning, bleary-eyed and hungover, Roy renewed his commitment. "This week, I'll stop drinking."

But each weekend found Roy in an alcoholic stupor once more, followed by another vow to stop drinking. After several weeks of hollow promises, Steve had enough of the lies.

"I'm going to stop drinking," Roy said again. This time, Steve didn't let the comment slide by.

"Who are you kidding, Roy?" Steve said, exasperated. "You'll *never* stop drinking."

Roy's anger flared. For a couple of months he stewed, his resentment toward Steve building. He hated that Steve didn't believe he was capable of quitting the booze. *I'll show him,* he finally thought. From that moment on, not a drop of alcohol passed Roy's lips.

Although Roy's demeanor improved after he sobered up, the real change in Roy's life came shortly afterward. He swallowed his pride and told Steve that he needed help. Steve took him to a lecture held by a professor of the Western Seminary in Sacramento, a graduate school that taught those pursuing a career in Christian ministry. Roy was at the end of his rope, and the words the professor spoke to the crowd hit him in the heart: "Tonight, go into your room, close the door, kneel on the floor at the foot of the bed, and tell God everything you've done wrong. Don't hold anything back, but tell him everything."

When Steve and Roy went home, Roy did exactly that. He poured out his heart to God, recounting every detail of the immorality he'd committed, sharing the pains and hardships of his life, and asking Jesus to be his savior and lord. In the morning, Roy felt as if a great weight had lifted from him. His life wasn't perfect, but he was heading down the right track at last. He was finally able to begin healing from the pain of years of abuse and ridicule as he learned to forgive those who had mistreated and emotionally injured him throughout his life.

The upward trend continued as he learned to read, encouraged by Glenys and the preacher of the church Roy began attending, Pioneer Presbyterian. Roy's first teacher was Gary Fick, who later went on to teach at Cornell University. After Gary moved to New York, Roy's instruction was taken over by Mae Martin. After months of studious learning, Roy read Psalm 118:24 in front of the congregation: "This is the day the LORD has made; let us rejoice and be glad in it."

Truly it was a day to rejoice. Roy had been told his entire life that he was too stupid to ever learn to read, but at the age of fifty he was proving his critics wrong. It was becoming apparent that what Roy had truly been overcoming his entire life was not his learning disability, but rather people's rock-bottom expectations of him.

Although Glenys died in 1991, leaving the bachelor brothers alone in the family house, Roy's determination to read did not die with her. He continued his studies under the tutelage of other ladies, including Sybil Anderson and Jean Harvey.

The transformation from the bitter drunk to the beloved town celebrity was complete. In 1995, Roy was ordained as a deacon at Pioneer Presbyterian Church, where he began serving the community by visiting with housebound elderly, telling stories during the children's service at church, and reading passages from the Bible aloud. Roy made amends with his baby brother and worked at Lester Farms Bakery, where he kept the place tidy and greeted everyone who came through the door. Even the high school janitor, who had treated Roy so cruelly, came to see Roy in a new light.

"I'm sorry for how I treated you. I know it was wrong," he told Roy. "Will you forgive me?"

"I already did," Roy replied. It was Roy's ability to forgive those who had mistreated him that allowed him to heal from the past wounds and move on.

And the happiness that radiated through Roy was infectious. Everywhere he went, people smiled and returned his hugs. And on April 29 of 1995, the town honored him when they made him the Honorary Grand Marshall of the Youth Day Parade.

That day, as I rode my streamer-adorned bicycle down the parade route in my new hometown, I didn't see the man garbed in a brown suit who was being hailed by the crowd. Even if I had seen him, I wouldn't have known just how much of an impact he was going to have on my life. I didn't know that Roy was going to touch the hearts of many students, including me, or that he was going to have a positive, lasting impact on the community of Winters and the children of the surrounding towns. But it was on that day, when Mom first noticed the small-town celebrity, that our futures began to intertwine.

Chapter 2
Red Tail Farm

WHEN MY FAMILY moved to Winters in the spring of 1995, Roy was already a prominent figure in town. But there was something missing in his life. Working at the Grosse Pointe Hunt Club as a young man had left him with a lifelong passion for horses, and he took every opportunity available to visit ranches and interact with the gentle giants. But he was limited to petting the horses through fences and watching them from a distance, and that wasn't enough for him. He wanted more.

What Roy didn't know was the foundation was being laid for the unexpected fulfillment of his aspiration. As fate would have it, my parents' decision to move to a rural community was driven by the desire to establish a horse ranch. Mom had a dream of raising and training horses, which was motivated by her passion for the majestic animals.

Their quest led them to Yolo County and the town of Winters, which was less than an hour's commute to work at Kaiser in Vallejo for Dad. But a new medical clinic was planned to open in Vacaville, only twenty minutes from Winters, and Dad quickly put his name down on the list to transfer to the new facility when it was scheduled to open in 1996. After looking at countless country properties, both those with and without a house or barn, they decided on a forty-eight-acre parcel of farmland devoid of any buildings or trees.

Their new land was located near the western edge of the patchwork of squares and rectangles that comprise the cultivated agricultural land of Yolo County, just a few miles from the rolling foothills of the oak-crowned Coastal Range. On clear days, the jagged, snow-covered tops of the Sierra Nevada Mountains were visible far to the east, with the solitary peak of Mount Diablo to the south and the Sutter Buttes, the world's smallest mountain range, making a bump on the northern horizon. Spread out between the mountains and hills was mile after mile of flat, open fields, where everything from wheat and corn to walnuts and almonds were grown. Unhindered by natural formations, most roads bisecting the rural lands were sequentially numbered straight lines exactly a mile apart, making it incredibly difficult to get lost.

While they were planning their dream ranch, Mom purchased a three-year-old Fox Trotter filly named Tomboy—the first horse of her own and the first mare of the future breeding ranch. Mom had decided to raise Missouri Fox Trotters because the breed was renowned for a smooth gait and calm disposition. Not long after she bought her first horse, Mom and Dad went to Missouri to find mares and fillies to serve as the foundation for their herd. Their purchases ranged from immature fillies just reaching breeding age to proven mares with foals at their sides and another on the way.

My parents rented a house in town while construction was underway at Red Tail Farm, named in honor of the red-tailed hawks that frequently swooped over the fields. The barn was completed before the house, in order to accommodate the handful of horses ready to be brought from the Show-Me State in the trailers of professional haulers.

The barn was relatively basic compared to many stables. One hundred feet long and forty feet wide, it was simply a blue, peaked metal roof set atop twenty-foot wooden poles, with an enclosed tack room to store saddles and bridles at one end. The narrow ends, which faced due north and south, had walls and large, sliding doors to protect the horses from the wet southern winds that bring rainstorms through the area and the howling, dry northern winds that tear down trees. Since there is rarely a crosswind from the east or west, the long sides of the barn were left open. The center aisle of the barn was twelve feet wide, with pipe-panel stalls extending out both sides.

At the southern end of the barn were larger, oval outside corrals, which were connected to the southeast stall by a series of gates, making it simple to turn the horses out by herding them as a group rather than catching them individually.

One of the outside corrals also had a large gate leading to an irrigated pasture for the horses, which was divided into spacious sections by white electric fence. When the ground was dry, the horses could be turned out twice a day to graze on the pasture rather than being fed hay, which both cut down on the feed bill and gave the horses an opportunity to frolic and play in a large area.

Almost immediately after the main structure of the barn was finished, Mom took my brother, Brian, and me to the Yolo County Animal Shelter to get a pair of kittens. Mom's policy on cat adoption was that we always had to get at least two, so that the kittens would have a friend to play with as they got accustomed to their new home. When one of our cats died, we got two new kittens, so as the years went by, despite the fact that all our cats were spayed and neutered, our barn cat population still multiplied, finally peaking at fifteen. The first two kittens were an orange tabby I named Tiger and a black fluff-ball Brian named PJ.

Not long after we brought the kittens home, my parents set up the pipe-panel corrals, leaving Brian and me to entertain ourselves. Typical of any mischievous eight-year-old, Brian's favorite game was taking Tiger and PJ into the tack room and playing with them while I was locked outside. Unfortunately for him, this game of tease-the-little-sister backfired one day.

"I can't get out!" Brian's voice came faintly through the thick metal door. "The lock wouldn't twist, and when I tried to use pliers to open it, it broke off!"

"Okay, I'll get the key from Mom and Dad!" I yelled back.

I raced down the barn aisle and outside, where Mom and Dad were lifting the heavy fencing in the nearly one-hundred-degree heat.

"Mom! Mom! Can I have the key to the tack room? Brian's locked in!"

"No, he's not. He's just teasing you," Mom said, trying to placate me.

"No, he really is! Can't I just have the key?"

"No. Now leave me alone. I'm busy."

Dejected, I returned to the tack room with the bad news. "Mom won't give me the key. Are you sure you can't open the door?"

"Yes, I'm sure! Go get the key. Tell her I'm locked in."

I dutifully trotted back to where my parents were working.

"Mom, Brian really is locked in. Can I please have the key?"

"Lauren, you don't need the key. I'm working. Please leave me alone."

"No, he really is—"

"Lauren, I'm not giving you the key."

Frustrated, I returned to my trapped brother. "Mom still won't listen to me!"

"Fine. I'll climb out the window."

"Okay, wait a minute. I'll get you something to climb down on."

The only window to the tack room was six feet off the ground. There were plenty of leftover construction materials lying around, so it didn't take much time for me to find a two-by-six plank long enough to create a slide from the window. Since there was gravel on the ground, I spread straw around to form a landing cushion in case Brian fell. Inside, he climbed on top of a counter, opened the window, and broke out the screen.

Just as Brian was about to make a triumphant slide down the board, Mom and Dad, sweaty and tired, arrived.

"What are you doing?" Dad asked, anger mounting as he saw the brand-new screen was broken.

"I *told* you! Brian's locked in the tack room."

Mom quickly intervened and took Dad aside before things got out of hand. "Lauren did tell us; we just didn't listen. We can't blame our kids for being resourceful. We should be thankful he didn't break his neck."

After that day, there weren't too many incidents of note as Red Tail Farm was constructed, until the long-awaited arrival of the mares. A huge horse trailer, towed by a semi-trailer truck, rolled to a stop in front of the barn at twilight. From inside came the sound of restlessly shifting hooves, the low nicker of mares, and the piercing, high-pitched whinnies of foals. The trailer swayed as horse after horse was unloaded: chestnut, bay, gray, even one brown-and-white pinto colt disembarked at their new home. The mares wore halters and were led by an attached rope, but the foals were free from any restraint. Despite this, they stuck close to their mothers' sides for safety, their eyes wide as they took in their new surroundings.

The ranch was still being built, but it was far enough along to house the horses. Water lines hadn't been completed to the barn, so for a few weeks the horses' water troughs were filled from a large water truck my parents rented. It wasn't much longer before construction on both the barn and the house was finally completed, and the Filarsky Family moved to Red Tail Farm.

The stage was set. All that was missing was one key player.

Chapter 3
First Encounter

ROY MADE HIS first visit to Red Tail Farm in the spring of 1999, when he was sixty-one and I was nine years old. At that time, the ranch was in full swing. Our fourth crop of foals was on the ground, our outside pens full of yearlings, two-year-olds, and three-year-olds. By then, I was beginning to master basic horsemanship skills on the back of my trusty gray pony.

Penny the pony had been an unexpected arrival at Red Tail Farm. When I was nearly eight, Mom started teaching me to ride on Rowdy, the big trail horse that she had bought for Dad, but Rowdy wasn't exactly the best mount for a child. He was so tall that I couldn't get my foot even close to reaching the stirrup to mount. Instead, in order to get in the saddle I had to scramble up the side of the horse like a monkey, using the saddle strings and rings for attaching saddlebags as handholds until I could reach the stirrup with my feet and grab ahold of the pommel with my hands.

The need for a small horse or pony for me to learn to ride was blatantly obvious when Mom trailered one of her young horses to a training clinic in the foothills of the Sierra Nevada Mountains. She brought me along so I could watch and learn.

The ranch where the clinic was held was a catastrophe. The owner fancied herself a horse "rescuer" and adopted horses that were destined for slaughter or had been taken from their owners due to abuse or neglect. The irony of her attempting to rescue horses was that almost all of the animals were in need of being rescued from her. The property was crowded with haphazard corrals containing skinny, worm-infested horses with untrimmed hooves. In the wild, horses will keep their feet worn down naturally to the correct length because they travel miles every day, but a domestic horse needs its hooves trimmed on a regular basis, much like cutting long fingernails. Long hooves are detrimental to horses; not only do they cause the horse to trip and stumble, but they can strain and damage muscles and tendons because they force the horses' hooves to awkward angles.

All the clinic attendees were horrified at the condition of the horses. The trainer leading the clinic was embarrassed; he spent his time traveling and teaching clinics at ranches across the country, and he was mortified to be in any way affiliated with that particular ranch. Unsurprisingly, it was the first and only time he held a clinic there.

As Mom and I walked through the ranch toward the arena, my heart ached to see the extent of neglect for the horses. Many stood with their heads held low in abject depression. Among the collection of horses was an old Shetland pony in a small corral by herself. Her gray coat was matted and had the coarse texture that is a hallmark of excessive worms living in a horse's gut. The outline of her ribs was visible, her worm-riddled belly was bloated with parasites, and the toes of her hooves were so long that they curled up like elf shoes.

Mom and I stopped for a minute outside of the pony's pen. The gleaming coat, lean muscle, and alert eyes of the filly Mom was leading only served to emphasize the poor health of the old mare before us. As we stood there, the ranch's owner quickly noticed my mom and me—the only child at the clinic—looking at the pathetic, despondent pony and came over to us.

"This is Penny. I got her from some people who didn't want her anymore because their kids outgrew her. She loves kids, and she would be great for your daughter."

Mom was leery. The pony looked like she was at Death's door, and even if Penny did recover her health, there was no telling if she would be a good mount for a child. Ponies are often the most cantankerous and ill-mannered of all equines.

Mom thought about poor little Penny throughout the clinic, while I went back to visit the pony when I got bored watching everyone else ride. In her shabby condition, Penny was far from the beautiful animal most girls imagine when they wish for their own pony, but I hoped that I would be able to have her, if only so she would get the care she clearly needed.

After the clinic was finished, Mom asked the trainer to take a look at the pony and evaluate her disposition. He obliged, taking Penny out of her dingy corral and working with her for a short while. As Penny moved around the arena, even at a walk, she continuously tripped on her overgrown hooves. The trainer decided that she was likely safe to ride— "Well, she seems gentle and willing. She may very well be more high-spirited when she feels better. I'd suggest you try her first, then let your daughter ride her once you know for sure she's a good pony."

He handed the lead rope to Mom and then boosted me onto Penny's bare back. Mom led Penny back to our trailer, with me clutching her mane to keep from being unseated by Penny's stumbles, and that day we loaded the pony in the trailer and brought her home to Red Tail Farm.

Based on the condition of Penny's teeth, our vet was able to determine that she was in her early thirties. Gray horses are not born white, but rather are born with any typical-colored coat with any markings—from black, bay, or chestnut to pinto, appaloosa, or roan—that gradually turns lighter as the horse ages, and the pony had finished turning pure white years before, save for a pair of unusual palm-sized copper-colored spots on either side of her withers. It was from those two circular patches that Penny got her name.

Fortunately for Penny, Mom remembered a story that she had heard from a fellow equestrian who had purchased a severely worm-infested horse years before. When the horse's new owner gave the animal a normal dose of deworming medicine, the massive die-off of worms caused the horse to die of toxic shock, to the owner's disbelief and regret. Instead of giving Penny a full dose of dewormer, Mom gave her a quarter of the amount of medicine recommended for an equine equal to Penny's weight. Even that small amount caused Penny to feel ill for a few days, but it wasn't life-threatening. Mom continued to give Penny small doses of wormer every few weeks until the pony was finally rid of the parasites. Luckily the first round of deworming was the hardest on Penny, and she didn't get sick again from the repeated treatments.

In the same manner, Penny's hooves couldn't be returned to normal with one trim. The long toes caused the angle of the hoof walls to change drastically, and to prevent Penny from being injured by a substantial alteration to her hooves, the farrier returned every two weeks to change the hoof angle a few degrees each time, until finally properly shaped hooves replaced the deformed "elf shoes" Penny had when we first laid eyes on her.

Once Penny was finally healthy and sound, Mom rode her to see if the pony was as gentle as she had acted while sick. Penny had livened up quite a bit, but the renewed vigor with the return of her health revealed a sweet and merry little pony. Brian and I immediately started riding her all over the ranch. Penny was a great pony for a kid; she was always friendly and happy, and she never bucked while being ridden. While she was old, she still had more than enough energy to trot and gallop everywhere, especially back toward the barn if her rider fell off.

Despite her strong spirit and vigor, Penny was still old and small, and her riders were growing every year. By the time I turned nine, I was ready for a younger, bigger horse, and Penny was ready for a quiet life of semi-retirement. Dad knew a couple who had a horse-crazy daughter and a severely handicapped son; they were looking for a pony to pull a cart so their daughter could take their son for rides. We had been told that Penny was trained to drive, so we gladly gave her to them. Penny lived out the rest of her years under their loving care, while I started riding Damien, an old Paso Fino given to me by Grandma Lulu when she decided to buy another horse.

Damien was a small horse, about fourteen and a half hands; he was the perfect size for a growing adolescent. His coat was cherry bay—rich red-brown, with a black mane and tail. He had black legs with white socks on both hind legs. His face had a palm-sized white star with a narrow stripe that widened as it ran down his face, touching the inner rim of each nostril. His right eye had a light blue, cloudy ring of scar tissue from getting poked by a stick while out on pasture when he was a foal. He wasn't blind in that eye, but his vision was impaired, and he compensated for it by going down the trail with his head cocked to the right so he could see what was in front of him more clearly with his good left eye. Dad always joked that Damien was "blind in one eye and can't see out of the other."

After receiving Damien, I became a member of the Winters 4-H horse group, where I was able to learn more about the basics of horsemanship and had the opportunity to participate in fun events such as camping with our horses at Point Reyes National Seashore, competing in horse shows, and spending time with other equestrians in various social activities.

One such gathering was a barbecue, which Mom hosted at Red Tail Farm. A few days before the event, the mother of another girl in the group asked Mom if it was okay to bring Roy out to help with the barbecue.

In the four years that had passed since the Youth Day Parade, Mom had seen Roy around town frequently and would stop to say hello to him, but did not yet consider him her friend. At that time, Roy worked at Lester Farms Bakery in town, where Mom occasionally went to get coffee and a pastry in the morning after dropping Brian and me off at school.

The first time that Mom went to the bakery, she saw Roy mopping the linoleum floor. She immediately recognized the man from the parade and was surprised to see him working as a janitor.

Roy had never seen her before, but he welcomed her with a smile and said, "Hello! How are you doing?"

"I'm fine, thanks. How are you?" Mom replied.

"Fine, fine. I'm Roy. What's your name?" Roy asked.

"My name is Cheryl," Mom responded, as she returned Roy's warm handshake.

"Pleased to meet you, Cheryl," Roy said. "Don't worry, I won't keep you. You go ahead and order."

Mom stepped up to the counter as Roy went back to mopping the floor. After she had received her donut, she headed to the door.

"You have a good day, now," Roy called out.

"Thanks! You do the same." Mom left with a smile that had nothing to do with the sugary treat she was carrying.

Mom encountered Roy on several other occasions, usually when she and I stopped for a donut on the way to go trail riding or to a show. Mom always parked the horse trailer on the street outside the bakery while we went inside, and the big white trailer drew Roy like a moth to a flame. He peppered Mom with questions about the horses and sometimes asked to see them, which she usually obliged. Roy would give their noses a pat through the metal bars of the windows. He missed the horses he had cared for at the Hunt Club, and he took any opportunity to interact with a horse.

But a quick touch through a window is a poor substitute for a meaningful encounter, and the 4-H barbecue was finally giving Roy the opportunity to visit our horses at Red Tail Farm.

An overcast sky and continuous drizzle were not enough to dissuade us from having our barbecue. Instead, we moved everything under the shelter of the barn, using hay bales as seats and tables.

While Mom's intention was to have Roy help cook the burgers and hot dogs, her plans had to change since Roy was afraid of the fire. So instead Mom cooked while Roy wandered down the barn aisle, mesmerized by the horses. At the north end were the six broodmares, their foals by their sides, sheltered from the rain in their own stalls. From sweet DeeDee to old Lady Gray, the mares and their offspring were all curious and friendly, more than willing to stick their heads through the rails and nuzzle Roy as he walked down the barn aisle.

At the far southern end of the barn was Magic Duke, our new stallion. For the prior two years, Mom had trailered her mares to a ranch near the Oregon border in order to breed them to Duke. When Duke was put up for sale, Mom immediately bought him. His bloodlines were impeccable; the grandson of the 1985 Missouri Fox Trotter World Grand Champion,

Black Cloud C., he had great conformation and disposition. To top it all off, Duke was a solid black stallion, Mom's dream horse. What Mom didn't know was that Duke was actually homozygous for the black color gene, which meant that he would pass on his ebony color, or a variation of it depending on the mare's genetics, to all of his offspring.

Mom warned all visitors at Red Tail Farm to stay at least three feet from Duke's pen. We never had an incident where Duke misbehaved, but owning a stallion is somewhat akin to owning a bear or a lion. The testosterone pumping through their system makes even tame and gentle studs inherently dangerous, and it only takes a split second for a stallion to rip muscle from bone, tear off an arm, or strike with lethal force.

The only other horses that visitors couldn't pet that day were the yearlings, two-year-olds, and three-year-olds, though it was the weather that kept people away. The young horses splashed in the mud of the outside paddocks, nipping and playing with each other despite the rain, their shaggy winter coats keeping them warm and cozy in the wet weather.

All the horses in the barn, no matter what age or gender, came to the fence and begged to be petted—all except one.

Rowdy, a tall chestnut gelding with a white star on his forehead, stood at the far end of his stall, in the rain, even though he could have come under the shelter of the barn roof.

"Come here, boy," Roy said, stretching his arm through the bars of the pipe-panel fence.

The reddish-brown gelding stood stiff, his head up and ears pricked forward at Roy, but with a touch of fear in his eyes.

"Hey, horse," Roy said.

Rowdy didn't move.

Finally Roy wandered back down the barn aisle, leaving the standoffish horse alone. Rowdy watched him leave, still standing in the rain.

In its own way, Rowdy's upbringing had been as hard as Roy's. He was abused as a colt, ridden by a heavy-handed cowboy who used spurs to constantly jab the young horse on to greater and greater speeds. Rowdy learned early in life that humans were the source of pain, and he flinched when touched, even when it was just a gentle caress. When he saw a person carrying a stick, he would quiver and stay as far from them as possible, afraid that he was going to be beaten with it.

Mom found Rowdy when she was searching for a riding mount for Dad, who needed a horse that was tall, strong, and gentle. At first it seemed that Rowdy only fit the first two requirements, but his new owner, who had rescued Rowdy from abuse, finally convinced Mom that Rowdy was what she was looking for.

"He'll take care of you," the man promised.

And so Mom brought Rowdy home to Red Tail Farm. For the first few weeks, the gelding refused to walk while being ridden. Any slack in the reins was considered a cue to speed up, so Mom rode him at a canter around the perimeter of the ranch until he was tired enough to walk, and she praised him for it. Slowly but surely, Rowdy learned that it was good to simply walk—that spurs wouldn't dig into his sides the moment he slowed—and he began to marginally relax.

Even though he bore emotional scars from his past, Rowdy was indeed a horse that would take care of his rider. He was surefooted and smooth, and he tackled any obstacle on the trail—from fording rivers to climbing steep mountains—with ease. He was unafraid of the wildlife we encountered, but he trembled when we happened upon other people.

Mom and I took Rowdy and Damien to a poker ride, a trail ride where people handed each rider a playing card at certain places along the trail. At the end of the ride, the riders submitted the cards they collected during the ride, and prizes were awarded to those with the best poker hands.

When we reached the first card stop, a man was waiting on the tailgate of a pickup truck. He had a deck of cards in his hand, and he stood up as we rounded the bend in the trail and came into sight. Mom rode Rowdy toward him to get her card; I followed on Damien, his short legs moving quickly to keep up with Rowdy's long stride.

As Mom approached the man standing next to the trail, he held up a card for her to take as she rode by. Rowdy immediately halted, looking in alarm at the man holding a strange object. Mom gave Rowdy a nudge with her heels to ask him to move forward, but Rowdy stepped sideways as he moved, crunching through a few small bushes as he avoided the card-wielding cowboy.

"Whoa!" Mom commanded, pulling Rowdy to a stop. She reached out to take the card as the man walked toward Rowdy's side. Rowdy sidestepped again, staying just out of reach.

"Maybe try walking toward him from the front," Mom suggested as she pulled Rowdy to a stop once again. The man stepped back and circled around to approach Rowdy's head; the horse responded by backing away in fright.

After several more unsuccessful attempts to get a card, Mom gave up and had the man hand her card to me instead. Damien stood perfectly still while I took two cards, one for me and one for Mom, and put them in my saddlebags. At the rest of the stops, I always ended up having to take Mom's card as well as my own because Rowdy refused to allow the person on the ground near him.

Despite Rowdy's deficiencies, he soon became Mom's number-one riding mount—when she wasn't on a youngster that she was training, of course—and only seldom did he serve his intended purpose as Dad's steed. Brian outgrew his desire to ride horses at the same time he outgrew Penny, and Dad never had much enthusiasm for riding more than a few times a year. Consequently, it took a fair bit of convincing to get one of the men in the family on a horse, so usually it was just Mom on Rowdy and me on Damien.

Damien was in the barn when Roy was greeting all the horses, and the little bay horse gave Roy a once-over, snuffling his clothes in a quest for hidden carrots or cookies. Grandma Lulu had spoiled Damien with treats, so he always searched people's pockets. If they had been at the Hunt Club, Damien might have succeeded in finding a snack, but unfortunately for the greedy gelding, Roy hadn't brought a gunnysack full of carrots.

Food was ready by the time Roy finished petting all the horses, and we all sat down to a hearty meal of hamburgers, hotdogs, baked beans, and chips. Afterward, Roy said goodbye to all the horses and made one more attempt to pet Rowdy through the fence. He was unsuccessful.

Rowdy stayed out in the rain, watching Roy with mistrust. To the horse, Roy was just another person who might hit and abuse him. Rowdy had no idea that Roy had experienced similar abuse—and worse, emotional abuse—and could empathize with his fear.

Chapter 4
Christmas Presents

AFTER THE BARBECUE at Red Tail Farm, Mom saw Roy in town on a fairly regular basis, either as he shuffled from his house to Eagle Drugstore, where he sat outside on a bench and greeted the passers-by, or when he was sweeping the floors at Lester Farms Bakery. One Saturday morning, Mom's friend Carol met her at the bakery for an early lunch, where they sat next to a window and talked.

Mom looked out of the window and saw Roy hosing down the sidewalk. When he looked up from his task, she waved at him. In return, Roy lifted the hose and sprayed the glass, pretending to soak the two women. Mom smiled, causing Roy to laugh like a little boy teasing his sisters.

When Roy finished with his job, he came inside to give Mom a proper greeting. She stood up to give him a hug—Roy accepts nothing less than a hug from someone he likes—and introduce him to Carol.

"Carol, Cheryl, the names are almost the same. No wonder you two are friends," Roy said with a laugh. "Cheryl, I was just wondering—tomorrow I'm going to speak to the children in church, and I wanted to invite you to come." Ever the gentleman, he turned to Carol. "You would be more than welcome to come too."

"Thank you, Roy, but I live a long way from here," Carol replied. "I go to church near my house."

"Cheryl, do you want to come?" Roy asked again.

Mom was torn; our family didn't attend church, but she could see how important it was to Roy. "Yes, Roy, I'd be delighted to come to see you speak at church. I'll bring the kids. Bruce is on-call tonight, so he can't come."

And so the next day, Brian and I found ourselves seated on either side of Mom in the hard wooden pews, bowing our heads for prayer and standing to sing unfamiliar hymns. Before the pastor's message, he invited all the children to come to the front for Roy's story. As all the regular-attendee children walked forward, Brian and I remained in our seats; he was too stubborn and I was too shy to go to the altar.

Roy ambled to the front, where the children sat on the steps leading to the pulpit, and began his story. "When I was your age, kids weren't always nice to me. After school, one of the things we'd do is play baseball. How many of you like to play baseball?" Several small hands went up.

"Well, after school we'd get together and pick teams. And the two captains would pick who they wanted on their team. First he would pick, and then the other one, and so on until everyone was on a team.

"But nobody picked me; they didn't want me to play with them.

"So you know what I did? When they started to play without me, I went, and I sat on the bench, and I cried. And you know, it hurt, it hurt that nobody wanted me."

Roy paused to look at the children. "Everybody needs friends, even retarded people. So be nice to one another. And I want you to know that I love you, and Jesus loves you."

At the end of his story, the children returned to their seats, and the pastor walked up to the pulpit to deliver the sermon. After the service, the congregation had coffee and pastries in the adjoining hall. Roy immediately sought our family out to thank us for coming and to invite us to come to church again.

"We'll see," Mom hedged, unwilling to make a further commitment at the time.

The next time that I saw Roy was when I was on my way to my first 4-H horse show. Mom and I stopped at the bakery to get a special treat for breakfast.

"How are you doing?" Roy asked as he gave me a hug.

"Good!" I replied, nerves buzzing in anticipation of my first competition. "I'm going to ride Damien in my first show today."

"Wonderful!" Roy said. "I'm sure you'll have a lot of fun and do great. Just remember though, to always get up and try again if something goes wrong. I knew a girl once who fell off her horse the first time I saw her riding. She rode her horse right at a jump, and right before the jump her horse stopped, but she didn't. She went flying off right over its head. She went over the jump, but the horse didn't. But she got right back on, and the next time, the horse did the jump."

"Okay, thanks, Roy," I said. Little did I know that I was about to receive a similar experience.

Once we arrived at the arena where the show was being held, I started getting Damien tacked up. I had spent the day before giving Damien a bath and cleaning his saddle and bridle in preparation for the show. Once he was ready, I changed into my show clothes: clean jeans and a brand-new white shirt, which I had left hanging in the tack room of the trailer until Damien was ready so that it wouldn't get dirty. I then mounted up and rode into the arena to warm up.

The arena was filled with horses and riders. Most of them were older than me: seasoned veterans of the 4-H, who had ridden in many shows. I was one of the youngest riders, but since the show classes were split up into beginner, junior, and senior levels, I was going to be competing against the other girls who were close to my age.

But despite the fact that there were several girls my age in the arena, I stood out from the rest of the crowd because of my horse. Damien was a Paso Fino, the only gaited horse in the entire ring. All of the other competitors rode non-gaited horses, such as Quarter Horses, Paints, Appaloosas, and Arabians, making Damien stand out as an oddity, with his rapidly churning "eggbeater" gait in sharp contrast to the steady one-two, one-two march of all the trotting horses.

As Damien and I gaited around the arena, I realized how much of a disadvantage I had. Damien's legs moved rapidly up and down, but each stride was very short lengthwise, meaning that the other horses trotted much faster than he did. We had no chance of winning any of the speed events, such as pole bending or barrel racing. And since Damien didn't have the same style of trot as at the other horses, we were going to get low marks from the judges in classes like western pleasure, where our movements were being judged.

My veins were flooded with adrenaline from anxiety and trepidation as the arena cleared out in preparation for the first western pleasure class. It was the class for beginners, so when it began, Damien and I re-entered the ring with a half-dozen competitors. Damien pranced with excitement, feeling the tension in my body as we circled the big, sandy stadium. The stands were mostly empty, with only a couple dozen parents watching the show, but to me it felt like being on display before a packed Super Bowl stadium.

By the time we reached the judge's stand, Damien decided he needed to release some of the tension that he was picking up from me. He dropped his head and bounced in the air, crow-hopping in front of the judges. He didn't buck very high or hard, but with how stiff I was, it was more than enough to send me crashing to the ground, scraping my chin on the rough sand. Damien continued to frolic around the arena, leaving me behind to attempt to salvage my pride.

As I stood up, a few tears trickled down my face—not from the injury, since I had fallen harder before, but from the humiliation of falling off in front of everyone at my very first show. My once-pristine shirt was brown with dirt, and my helmet had a scratch on its smooth surface.

By the time I got up, one of the adults caught Damien and led him to the arena gate, where Mom was waiting to give me a hug and encouragement. I didn't get back on Damien, who to my fury was looking perfectly smug and pleased with himself, but instead retreated to our horse trailer in embarrassment, dreading my next event, which was due to start an hour later.

My savior that morning was Amanda, one of the high school girls in my 4-H club. She saw how upset I was and pulled me up on the back of her gentle Arabian, Hanaad. Together, we rode Hanaad around the trailer parking area, with me sitting behind the saddle and clinging to Amanda's waist for balance. After a while, my confidence was restored and my embarrassment was put far enough behind me that I remounted Damien and returned to the show ring for the rest of my classes.

As expected, Damien and I consistently came in last, but at least he did not crow-hop again, and I stayed in the saddle for all the events. We jigged through poles and paso trotted around barrels, clocking in dismally slow times. But Damien had no idea that we were losing at anything. Instead, he hummed to himself, a quirky habit that he exhibited whenever he was happy, and listening to him "sing" lifted my spirits and brought back my trust in my little horse.

But it was in the last competition of the day that he and I were vindicated for our disastrous debut and all our losses. It was called the Dollar Bill Ride, and it was the only event in the show that had a cash prize. It was also the only part of the show in which a gaited horse could truly excel.

For the Dollar Bill Ride, all the contestants took off their horses' saddles and rode bareback. A dollar bill was placed under each rider's thigh, with a few inches sticking out from the back of their leg. The riders circled around in the arena, following the announcer's commands: walk, trot, canter, turn the other direction, and make a circle. If the dollar fell to the ground, the rider was "out" and had to stop in the middle of the arena, while a person on the ground collected the fallen dollar.

The competition included all age ranges, from the young beginners like me, who were only allowed to walk and trot, to the older juniors and seniors, who were required to canter while the beginners continued to trot. At the end, the last beginner and the last junior or senior rider to still have their dollar under their leg split the cash prize of all the losers' dollars—around forty dollars in all. Even though the jackpot was shared, it was a lot of money for a nine-year-old.

As all the riders spaced themselves along the rail in the arena, I was nervous and excited. After a day of loss after loss due to my horse, I knew that for once Damien and I had a strong competitive edge. After all, not only was I more accustomed to riding him bareback, since at home I rarely bothered to put a saddle on my mount before I rode, but Damien's smooth gait would make it easier to keep my legs firmly pressed against his side.

As the contest started and we walked around the edge of the arena, I squeezed Damien tightly with my thighs, glancing down every few steps to check that my dollar bill was still in its place. Then the judge commanded us to trot, and I urged Damien forward into a paso trot. I was barely jostled as Damien hummed and happily gaited around the arena, while all around the arena the other competitors clung to their trotting horses' manes and bounced like they were riding pogo sticks, their own dollar bills falling to the ground in a green rain.

Soon there were fewer than a dozen riders left trotting along the rail with their dollars still hanging on precariously. The judge ordered the older riders to canter, which allowed me to see how many other beginners were left for me to defeat. Only two other horses remained at a trot, and as I watched, one of their dollars fell to the ground, leaving just one other beginner besides me.

Cantering caused the older riders to lose their dollars at a quicker rate, and before long there was only one senior rider left. She was allowed to halt her horse in the center of the arena, while the last beginner and I continued to strive for first place. I peeked down at my dollar and saw that it was beginning to slip. Even Damien's smooth gait wasn't entirely bump-free, and the dollar was slowly emerging from underneath my leg. I squeezed my knees tighter, determined to outlast my rival, and at last I heard the judge announce, "That's the last dollar. We have our winners!" I looked down again, hardly able to believe it. My dollar was still there. I had won at last.

At all the other shows I attended, the only event I looked forward to was the Dollar Bill Ride; my victories in that contest were made all the sweeter by all of my bitter defeats the rest of the day and by the folding green I got to stick in my pocket at the end.

Damien's personality reflected the highs and lows that I experienced at shows with him: he was a reliable mount for a child (the only time he ever bucked was at our first show), but he also had an impish, mischievous personality that showed through in his relationships with other horses. Some of his behavior was driven by the fact that he was gelded late in life. Most male horses are castrated when they are approximately one year old, but Damien had been a stallion until the age of ten. Although he never exhibited any dangerous or stallion-like behavior with humans, he wanted to be the boss of the herd.

One time, Damien escaped by rubbing his halter off over his ears while he was tied at the hitching rail. He immediately pranced down the barn aisle to the outside pen that held Duke. Arching his neck and whinnying like a stallion, Damien danced around the perimeter, challenging Duke for position as top stud. Duke tossed his head, pinned his ears, and lashed out, frustrated that he couldn't reach his rival. The ebony stallion bellowed a challenge at the little bay gelding, daring him to fight through the bars of the fence, but Damien was smart, staying just out of reach of the larger horse, clearly taunting Duke as if he were saying, "Look at me out here. You can't get me!"

As the smallest adult horse on the ranch, Damien wasn't so lucky if he was in a paddock with other animals, since they didn't let him get away with his posturing as alpha male. Initially we put him out on the pasture with Rowdy, since generally geldings get along better with one another than they do with mares. But Rowdy quickly grew tired of Damien's attitude, and he decided to put pesky Damien in his place by kicking and biting him. In the end, Damien resorted to running through the hot-wire fence to escape when his plan to dominate the larger gelding drastically backfired. After that incident, we kept Damien separated from the other horses.

Damien got his revenge on Rowdy at every available chance. When Mom and I rode, Rowdy was in front, setting the pace with his long strides. Damien tagged behind, alternating walking and gaiting to keep up. Every time he gaited, Damien tried to sneak as close to Rowdy's hindquarters as possible. Then he would snake his head forward and chomp down. While most horses would have kicked the horse behind them, Rowdy's well-mannered side shone through, and he never tried to kick Damien, despite the numerous times he was bitten while I was learning to control the impish Paso Fino.

The unusually mild attitude of Rowdy under saddle, combined with his reliable sure-footedness, was similar to the pony Fritz in Mom's favorite children's book, *Fritz and the Beautiful Horses,* by Jan Brett. Fritz is a little shaggy pony who was scorned by the tall, graceful horses and their young riders until a disaster occurred and the brave pony saved the day, winning him the everlasting love of the children and the respect of all the townspeople.

Fritz also reminded Mom of Roy, who, despite an early life full of derision from others, had retained a gentle heart and was beloved by an entire town. She decided that it was the perfect book for Roy to have and bought him a copy, which she left in her Suburban until the next time she saw him in town.

Roy was delighted by the book, and as a way of showing his thanks, he had Steve drive him to Red Tail Farm on the day before Christmas with a tray of dried fruits from Lester Farms for our family. Since we weren't home at the time, they left it on the front porch, a pleasant surprise upon our return. Mom immediately called Roy to thank him for the lovely and tasty gift.

During the course of the conversation, Mom asked Roy what his plans were for the holiday and found out that he and Steve were going to spend Christmas Eve with their good friend, and excellent cook, Sophie. But to Mom's surprise, Roy was going to be home alone on Christmas day. Steve had to work, driving a bus in Sacramento, and none of Roy's many friends in town had invited him to celebrate the holiday with them; in fact, Roy had been alone every Christmas since his mother died.

So on Christmas morning, after Brian and I had finished annihilating the wrapping paper under the tree, Mom drove to town to fetch Roy, who spent the day relaxing on our couch, sipping coffee while Brian and I showed off our Christmas loot. In the afternoon Roy, Mom, and I walked to the barn to give the horses a few tasty holiday treats of apples and carrots. The horses crowded the fence lines, jockeying for position with one another as they used their lips to snatch the morsels from our upturned palms. Even Rowdy came to the fence for a snack, stretching out his neck as far as possible so he could grab a quick bite from Roy's hand before retreating to the end of his stall, the delicacy not sufficient to lessen his apprehension of pain and abuse.

Chapter 5

Dance like Astaire

AFTER SPENDING CHRISTMAS at Red Tail Farm, Roy became part of the family, whether he was going grocery shopping with Mom or spending time out at the barn. Wherever he went, Roy was never far from a can of "blue pop," more commonly known as Diet Pepsi, which at the time was in a pale blue can. He wanted to learn to ride a horse, but Mom was too concerned about safety to allow it.

Safety was Mom's number one priority with the horses. "If you ever get in a situation where your horse is in danger, and the only way to help it is to put yourself in harm's way, it's better to let the horse die than to get injured trying to rescue it," Mom told me countless times when I was learning how to ride. It seems like a harsh statement, but horse lore is filled with tales of panicked horses crippling or killing those trying to help them. After all, it doesn't take much for an animal that weighs half a ton to do serious damage to a relatively puny human.

While the chances of encountering such a dangerous situation are slim—I have yet to be forced to choose my safety over my horse's—there was one unbreakable safety commandment that Mom instilled in me: Always wear a helmet when riding a horse. I fell off countless times when I was first learning to ride, mostly because I rode bareback everywhere. It didn't help that the equine I first learned to ride was Penny the pony, who had very slippery hair and was extremely fond of abruptly slowing from a canter, which was fast but easy to ride, to a choppy trot that would literally bounce any rider off her back. But despite my numerous falls, often smacking my head against the ground in the process, to this day I haven't received a head injury while riding because I always follow that rule.

With Roy, there were more safety concerns than a preventable head injury. Roy is prone to seizures that are initiated by sudden pain—simply stubbing his toe can launch one. Falling off a horse would most likely cause a seizure, something Mom wouldn't risk, even if it meant denying Roy his dream of riding.

Instead, Mom would bring out one of the older, gentle mares and let Roy brush it while she went about doing her chores of feeding and caring for the rest of the herd. Roy was nervous at first; he hadn't had much close contact with horses since his time working for the Grosse Pointe Hunt Club over thirty years earlier, and he was uncertain about how to even put a halter on a horse. But he had a gentle, reassuring manner, and he remembered the basics of horse safety.

One of the main safety concerns while working around a horse that is tied up is to not startle it. Horses are prey animals, and like any prey animal they have a "fight or flight" response to perceived danger. Some prey animals, like musk oxen, will form a protective circle when attacked by predators and use their strength and natural weapons of hooves and horns to fight. Others, like deer, simply try to outrun their assailant, relying on speed and maneuverability to avoid becoming dinner. Horses belong to the latter category, and despite their hard, sharp hooves that could seriously damage a predator, their instinct is to flee from danger.

A horse that is tied up doesn't have the option to run, so instead it may kick to defend itself. It is rare that a horse will maliciously kick a person, but horses easily sleep standing up, and a horse that is startled awake from its nap by a person making a loud noise or suddenly touching the horse from behind may reflexively kick. After all, it has nowhere to run to get away from the perceived danger.

Roy already knew about this danger with horses and how to properly conduct himself around them to prevent an accidental kicking. He was quiet and didn't make abrupt noises, talking softly and keeping a hand on the mare at all times to let her know where he was when he was in her blind spots. He worked slowly and methodically, brushing with the grain of the hair from head to tail. The placid mares loved the attention, licking their lips and sighing with contentment as they enjoyed a brief respite from their rambunctious foals.

After a few times of once-a-week horse grooming, Roy was eager for more. He had previously gotten the opportunity to ride Round Hill, an easygoing gelding at the Grosse Pointe Hunt Club, under the watchful eyes of both Red LaPearl, his boss, and Mary Steedman, a trainer and fellow stable hand who later went on to become a thoroughbred jockey. Roy rode in a small arena, Red watching from the outside and Mary in the center.

"Keep your knee bent," Mary told Roy.

"Straighten your leg," Red commanded.

So Roy accommodated them both, straightening his outside leg and bending the inside leg, riding cockeyed the whole time with nobody but Round Hill the wiser.

After moving to California, Roy had another opportunity to ride one day when he visited a ranch that raised horses for rodeos. Those horses weren't the animals used by cowboys to rope steers and herd cattle—they were the bucking broncos. Despite the fact that Roy always told people he would never ride a bronco, he leapt at the opportunity to actually do so. He clambered aboard, and the horse was let loose in the arena.

Roy didn't even feel the horse buck underneath him. One second, he was perched atop the horse's back, the next instant he was a featherless bird soaring through the air. Obeying all the laws of physics and gravity, Roy crashed to the ground, his pride and body both smarting. An iota of luck was with him that day, since he thankfully didn't have a seizure when he landed.

Although Roy didn't want to repeat the fine details of his jaunts atop Round Hill or the bronco, he was eager to get back in the saddle.

Mom, on the other hand, was still not keen on the idea of putting Roy on a horse. The best horse for a beginner rider is a so-called bomb-proof horse: a well-broke, gentle horse that doesn't buck or spook. Generally this translates to an older horse, a commodity that is in short supply on a breeding ranch. All the young horses, while destined to be steady mounts, were simply too green to put an inexperienced rider aboard. The result for Roy of that calamitous pairing would have been a fear of riding at best, hospitalization at worst; neither outcome was one that Mom looked upon favorably. And while the mares were older and gentle, they were always either heavily pregnant or with a foal at their sides. The only horse with a suitable mindset for Roy to ride was Damien, but the little gelding was simply too small to comfortably carry Roy.

The tension between Roy's pleading desire to ride and Mom's firm refusal on account of safety finally ended in a compromise: Mom offered to teach Roy how to train horses in the round pen, an occupation much less hazardous than riding but still challenging and capable of filling Roy's lifelong desire to work with horses. Our round pen is a circular arena sixty feet in diameter, with sand footing and six-foot-high pipe-panel fencing. The round pen is used for the initial training of a horse, to give it a strong foundation of training in preparation for being ridden.

One of the first lessons that Roy learned was how to hold the halter and put it on the horse. Some people leave the halter on all the time, so all they have to do is snap on a lead rope when they want to catch the horse, but this attempt to cut corners can end up having serious consequences. If a halter is left on a young, growing animal for too long, it can cut into the skin as the head outgrows its confines and, if still not removed, can permanently damage and reshape the bones in the skull. While this particular danger is not an issue with adults, the halter can get trapped on things such as fence posts, branches, or even the horse's own hind leg as it uses its hoof to scratch behind its ear in a manner similar to a dog scratching for fleas. When a horse becomes entangled, it sometimes panics in its struggle to free itself, often leading to a catastrophic wreck. Since we want to avoid any of those tragic outcomes, none of our horses wear halters in their stalls or paddocks.

There are two basic types of halters: web and rope. The most commonly used is a web halter because it fastens with a buckle, making it easy to put on the horse. Rope halters, as their name suggests, are made entirely of a thin, strong rope, with no metal buckles or rings like there are on a web halter. Rope halters are secured with a special knot instead of a buckle, which means they are more difficult for beginners to learn how to use. Unfortunately for Roy, he was going to have to use a rope halter in order to work in the round pen, since the lack of buckles meant the horse wouldn't be hit on the jaw with metal during certain training exercises.

First Mom had Roy practice tying the knot while hanging the halter on one of the tie rails instead of putting it on a horse, in order to allow him to learn one step at a time. Even with Mom's help, it was a frustrating experience for Roy as he learned to tie the knot—threading the rope through a loop, wrapping the end around the loop and then sticking it up through the space between the loop and the free end—while at the same time making sure the various parts of the halter were all in the right place. The knot had to be positioned so that it tightened on the loop; too high, and it would loosen while on the horse. The tension on the free end also had to be sufficient to hold the halter tight enough on the horse's head so the noseband didn't slip down. It was difficult to maintain that tension while focusing on tying the knot.

Once Roy had the basics of knot-tying mastered, he had to learn how to hold the halter. The lead rope had to be folded over his left arm, making sure there were no loops surrounding his arm or fingers. If there is a loop of rope, even a very loose one, around a person's limbs or digits and the horse attached to that rope pulls back, the loop will tighten, trapping that limb or digit, which could cause serious damage or even rip it off entirely.

The halter itself was held in the left hand, the noseband draped over the fingers with the neck strap on top. To put the halter on, first the right arm reaches around the top of the horse's neck to grab the neck strap from the left hand. The noseband is then slipped over the horse's muzzle and the right hand pulls on the neck strap to draw the noseband up the horse's face to its proper place, where it rests on sturdy bone rather than the easily-broken cartilage at the end of a horse's nose. The neck strap is then threaded through a loop at the top of the cheek piece, and the halter is tied in place.

After Roy figured out how to hold the halter, it was almost time for him to put it all together and catch a horse. But first, he took a halter home to practice flicking the lead rope up and down and wiggling it sideways in an S-shape to give different commands to a horse at the end of a long rope. Mom also sent Roy home with a video that covered the basics of round pen training so he could visualize and study what he was supposed to do and how the horse should respond.

The tape Mom gave to Roy was *The Noble Horse*, a National Geographic special that covered a wide variety of horse-related topics, from the horse culture of Mongolian nomads and their fifteen-mile-long races, to the refined teachings of the Spanish Riding School in Vienna and their "airs above the ground," the phenomenal aerial acrobatics performed by Lipizzaner stallions. The program also highlighted the wild roots of modern horses, from the Przewalski's horse in Mongolia, which is the only truly wild horse still alive, to Mustangs in the United States of America, which are feral descendants of horses brought over by Europeans centuries ago.

As part of the section on Mustangs, the video showed one way captured horses are trained. The featured trainer was Bryan Neubert, who specialized in starting young horses, either feral or domestic, under saddle. As part of Neubert's career, he also traveled to different locations and taught colt-starting clinics, in order to help horse owners start training and riding their own young horses. Mom had attended many of Neubert's clinics with her own colts and fillies, and had sent both our stallion, Duke, and a few batches of three-year-olds to Bryan Neubert's ranch for him to train.

In *The Noble Horse*, Neubert works with a young Quarter Horse stallion that was born on the open range and had never been touched by a person. In just three days of training, Neubert progressed from touching the horse to riding it in the arena and, finally, riding it outside the arena in the surrounding countryside.

The first day of Neubert's training was what was important for Roy to see. Neubert worked in the round pen with the stallion, moving slowly and deliberately, the horse focusing on him and reacting very sensitively to his changes in body position and posture. Neubert looked for the slightest change in behavior and smallest effort from the horse, and he rewarded that.

Since DVDs were not yet common, Steve copied the section of the VHS that showed Neubert so Roy could watch the round pen training multiple times without having to hassle with finding the correct spot on the tape.

Roy thrived watching the video. Decades earlier, he learned to dance by watching Fred Astaire and Ginger Rogers on the television and copying their moves. Roy practiced until he perfected his dance skills, which he showed off in the bars, "back in the days when I used to bend my elbow," as he describes it. And despite Roy's slow, deliberate movements most of the time, when he starts dancing, he taps into an unexpected grace and turns into a light-footed, nimble dancer.

It was a different kind of dance Roy needed to learn in order to be successful in the round pen, and he followed Neubert's every footstep on his living room floor, the curtains closed so people couldn't look in from the sidewalk and see what he was doing. Roy studied the way Neubert moved his body and scrutinized the way the horse responded. At one point, the camera followed over Neubert's shoulder as he approached the horse, allowing Roy to practically be in the pen with the horse, as if the horse was shifting from his own movements, not Neubert's. Roy watched the video every night for a week, until he had it practically memorized and knew the fundamentals of both round pen training and reading horse body language.

It was time to finally put what he had learned to practice.

The horse that Mom chose for Roy to work with was none other than Rowdy, who was trustworthy to not misbehave or accidentally bump into Roy. Rowdy's abusive upbringing also made him extremely sensitive to small gestures and acutely aware of every movement made by a human nearby. This made him ideal for responding precisely to commands given in the round pen, but it also created a challenge for a learner in that Rowdy would obey signals that the beginner had unknowingly and unintentionally given. Like anyone who has worked with animals, Roy soon learned that book knowledge or, in Roy's case, video knowledge, does not equate to experience. As with anything, round pen training was going to require hours of practice to perfect.

First Roy had to catch Rowdy, who stood at the back of his stall, eyeballing the two people opening his gate. Roy and Mom approached him slowly, one hand out to touch him as they walked toward his shoulder. Although Rowdy was a standoffish horse, he knew better than to try and walk away or turn so that his rear end was facing those trying to catch him. Mom told Roy how he should keep his eyes on Rowdy's shoulder rather than looking him straight in the eye, as direct eye contact can make horses nervous because they are prey animals.

Rowdy obediently lowered his stiff neck when Roy reached up to place the halter on him. Then he held still, tense but patient, as Roy fumbled to get the halter in its proper place with the knot tied correctly. Mom helped Roy make a few final adjustments, and they were ready. Roy led Rowdy and followed Mom, who carried the training flag, out to the round pen.

The flag used in round pen training doesn't look anything like what most people visualize when they hear the word "flag." Instead, it is a repurposed four-foot-long dressage whip, with a piece of a black trash bag—approximately a square foot—affixed to the end. The long length of the whip serves to extend the length of a trainer's arm, making it easier to direct the horse where to go, and the plastic bag functions as a noisemaker that lets the horse know the intensity of the command. It is not designed to scare or harm the horse, and while most horses are a little nervous at first about the flapping bit of plastic, they are gently touched all over their bodies with it until they get used to it and relax.

Once Roy released Rowdy in the round pen and was given the flag, Mom told him his goal for the day: "Be more interesting than horse manure."

Roy laughed at what he thought was a joke, but soon learned the truth to that instruction. As Roy stood talking to Mom, Rowdy walked around the sandy enclosure, head down as he inspected the piles of droppings left by horses that had been trained in the round pen previously. As with many animals, the scent of dung communicates information about an animal, such as gender and health. To horses, this is much more interesting than the person telling them to run around in a circle, and Rowdy ignored Roy and Mom as they talked at the gate.

Finally, Roy was ready to begin, and he took his place in the center of the round pen and flicked the flag, urging Rowdy to move. Rowdy complied, speeding around the enclosure at a brisk foxtrot. It soon became apparent that what Neubert made seem effortless in the video was in fact quite tricky. In order to get a horse to move forward in the round pen, the trainer must maintain a relative position behind the horse's shoulder, in effect driving the animal forward. If the trainer gets in front of the shoulder—despite being separated from the animal by about thirty feet— it acts to cut the horse off, causing them to stop or turn around. Likewise, if the trainer drifts too far behind the horse, the horse will feel a slack in the pressure and slow down or stop. It is all a matter of a few steps to the left or right as the horse circles around, and it was a frustrating experience for Roy to learn to maintain the proper balance of pressure placed at the correct point.

A mixed blessing about Rowdy was that he had been made to go fast his entire life. This meant that Roy didn't have to keep urging Rowdy to move, but it also meant that Rowdy refused to walk, and Roy had to learn to keep pace with the horse. There were many instances where Roy would misstep, causing Rowdy to skid to a stop and whip around in the opposite direction.

"The horse isn't being disobedient," Mom told Roy. "He just thinks you asked him to turn around. Don't worry, it takes practice. You'll get the hang of it."

As Mom had predicted, Rowdy also wanted to stop and smell the piles of manure when he felt a slack in pressure from Roy, who had to learn to predict where the horse would stop and prevent him from doing so by maintaining the pressure to move forward around the pen. Predicting when the horse would stop involved two basic factors: reading the horse's body language and knowing basic horse behavior. The former took practice and a keen eye for subtle changes, while the latter in this case involved a basic principle: Horses have very little imagination. If a horse stops to smell manure by the gate, he will likely try to stop at the same place on every lap, until he decides that the trainer is in charge and must be obeyed. Likewise, if a horse decides to cut across part of the pen to shorten the distance he has to run, he will do it at the same spot every time.

At first, this lack of imagination created a frustrating cycle: on every lap the horse would purposely be disobedient. But as Roy continued to learn to assert himself, Rowdy paid closer attention and settled down to work.

Another technique Roy had seen on the video and now needed to put into practice was how to ask the horse to stop. The method was to back away from the horse, relieving pressure and yielding a space that the horse was supposed to turn into, resulting in the horse coming to a halt with his body turned toward the center, facing the trainer. And while Rowdy knew what that command meant, it was difficult for Roy to execute, as it meant backing away from an animal that was moving in a circle, which meant the direction Roy was reversing had to fluctuate until Rowdy had come to a halt. If Roy didn't compensate for the movement of the horse around the pen, he would back too close to the opposite rail, effectively cutting Rowdy off once the horse reached the other side of the pen. When this happened, the meaning of the command changed from "turn and face me" to "turn around and go in the opposite direction."

Roy followed Mom's coaching for an hour, struggling to convey the proper commands to Rowdy. At last, after a particularly successful endeavor to ask Rowdy to halt, it was time for Roy to stop as well. The mid-afternoon sun was amplifying the call of air conditioning and a can of blue pop back at the house. And with any animal training, it is always best to end on a high note, so that the experience is rewarding for both animal and human. And despite the discouraging frustration at Roy's first hands-on lesson, the ice-cold cola had a slight aftertaste of victory.

Chapter 6
Kindred Spirits

AT THE SAME time Roy was learning to work with Rowdy in the round pen, I was ready to put round pen training to practical use for the first time. I had often helped Mom while she trained young horses, but I wasn't the primary trainer. Instead, I performed such tasks as sitting on the six-foot fence of the round pen and throwing my leg over the horse's back while Mom made the horse stand next to the fence, so it would get used to having a person above it, or I helped desensitize the horses Mom was riding by waving plastic bags or dragging objects around the horse.

Now that I was on the brink of turning twelve, however, I was eager to start training my filly, Delightful Cassie, who had been born on our ranch when I was nine years old. She was the daughter of my favorite mare, Cloud's Double Delight, who we called DeeDee. Cassie was one of only a few foals born on Red Tail Farm whose sire was not Duke, which meant Cassie was not black like almost all the other foals. Instead, she was a deep chestnut color, with a rich red coat and a mane and tail so dark that they almost appeared black. On her left hind leg was a white sock, and her forehead had somewhat unusual markings: a small star with a smaller white spot above it that we called a satellite. When she was born, I immediately fell in love with the dark red filly and begged Mom to let me have her as my own.

She said, "No."

I refused to accept that.

"You're too young to have a foal. You already have Damien."

"But I'll be twelve when she's ready to ride," I protested. "And Damien is getting old."

"Her back is too long," Mom countered.

"She'll grow into it. She's going to be tall."

Finally, whether she saw logic in my arguments or just gave in to my incessant nagging and begging, Mom said, "Yes."

Cassie was mine.

Though I didn't officially start training Cassie until two and a half years later, I constantly played with her, getting her accustomed to being handled, since at first she was skittish and afraid of people. DeeDee was one of the sweetest, gentlest horses alive, but when it came time to give birth, she was our sneakiest mare. Mares undergo several drastic physical changes in preparation for foaling: their entire back end—their hindquarters, tail, and lady parts—soften and loosen, until their tails are like limp dishrags, with no resistance to being picked up and swung around. Most importantly, within seventy-two hours of birth, a mare's udder will "wax," which means beads of fluid leak from their swollen teats and form stalactites on the tips, giving the appearance of dripping candle wax. With most mares, it is fairly easy to predict when the foal will be born based on the changes the mare undergoes.

But with DeeDee, it was different. She gave birth to four live foals while she lived at Red Tail Farm, and three of them were surprise babies that Mom found in the morning when she went out to feed the herd. Usually, Mom and I, and sometimes Brian, would spend the night sleeping in the back of the Suburban at the barn when a mare was due to give birth. We slept with the windows rolled down so the gushing sound of the mare's water breaking could wake Mom, and then we watched the foal being born, both to help the mare if necessary and so we could imprint train the foal.

Imprint training is a significant part of a foal's life. As soon as the baby came out, we would dry it off with towels, and then pet and rub it on every part of its body until it got used to our touch and stopped twitching. This process would form a bond between us and the foal, and it would teach the foal that humans are a part of its family, not predators that are going to hurt it.

Since we weren't around for Cassie's birth, she missed out on the vital imprint training. By the time we saw her in the morning, she was dry, which meant she had been born several hours earlier and had time to stand up, nurse, and begin to learn to run, even in the confines of a stall. And the two-legged creatures approaching her were unfamiliar, scary monsters in the eyes of the newborn filly. When we entered the stall, she skittered away and hid behind her mother.

I knew immediately that I wanted that foal, so I spent most of the day at the barn, chasing the then-unnamed filly around her stall, ducking around DeeDee in maneuvers that would have likely gotten me kicked by any other mare and catching Cassie. She weighed a little less than eighty pounds, about the same as me at the time, but she was still wobbly on her feet, so I was able to hang on as she struggled to get away. I scratched and petted the frightened filly until she calmed down and relaxed, teaching her that I was a source of love, not fear. Eventually, Cassie started coming to me of her own free will, wanting me to pet and rub her.

After I gained Cassie's trust, I started doing more things with her. I picked up her feet, held them, and tapped on them until she stood still, as she would need to in the future to get her hooves cleaned, trimmed, or shod. I put a tiny foal halter on her and led her around, brushed her, put her in the trailer, and accustomed her to scary things like flapping blankets and tarps. When she was a yearling, and Mom wasn't around, I even jumped on her back while she was loose in the pen, letting her walk where she pleased and get used to my weight—then light and scrawny— on her back.

My first surreptitious attempts at riding her didn't go so well. I led her to the hundred-gallon water trough in the pen, using nothing but my hands on her head to tell her where to go. Once she was in place, I carefully stepped up on the narrow rim of the trough, using Cassie to balance, grabbed her mane, and swung on. Cassie's head shot straight up in surprise, and she took off at a canter across the pen. I hung on, adrenaline pounding through my veins, until she veered toward the cluster of other yearlings in the corral with her. I didn't want to get kicked by one of them, so I swung off on the fly, landing hard but managing to keep on my feet. Cassie melted into the safety of the herd, snorting with fright.

One out-of-control ride wasn't enough to dissuade me. After all, I had learned to ride bareback on Penny the pony, who loved taking control and racing back to the barn, regardless of whether I was on her back, on the ground, or, in two cases, hanging on for dear life to the side of her neck, one knee clenched around her spine where I should be sitting, the other leg wrapped across her chest. I fell off more times than I could count, but after I was done crying in the dirt, I would always go catch the little gray pony, who had usually found a nice patch of grass or pile of hay to munch on as a reward for dumping her rider, and get back on. So having to jump off of Cassie wasn't that big of a setback, especially since I landed on my feet.

I walked over to Cassie and petted her to reassure her until she calmed down. Then I promptly led her back to the water trough to try again. At first, she sidestepped away from the water trough, preventing me from remounting. But every time she moved, I pushed her back over, until finally she stood still long enough for me to climb on again. After a few more times of racing across the pen, I stopped for the day, not wanting to hurt Cassie's growing tendons and bones. Or my own, since Cassie's fear-induced flight often led her on a collision course with the other yearlings, and they didn't appreciate being run into by the red filly with the crazy girl on her back and would occasionally aim a kick in our direction.

But one day of unauthorized training wasn't enough. Whenever I got the chance—whenever nobody was around to catch me—I jumped on Cassie's back, getting her used to the concept until she stood quietly or simply walked around the pen with me. Eventually, when Cassie was two, she would stand quietly and eat hay while I sat on her back, often holding and petting a chicken or cat while I did so. Mom saw me on those occasions, but since Cassie wasn't moving and I was always wearing a helmet, she didn't comment; it wasn't for another decade that I finally confessed the extent of my unauthorized training.

When Cassie was two and a half, the time most of our youngsters were starting training, my nagging began again. This time, I wanted to ride Cassie—officially, that is.

Once again, Mom said, "No."

Defeat slowly morphed into determination, until finally in the late summer of 2001, the day after I turned twelve, I walked up to Mom, saddle on my hip, and announced, "I'm going to ride Cassie. Are you going to be there or not?"

Mom saw that "No" was no longer an option; she always had a goal of raising her children to be as independent and resourceful as possible, which meant this declaration was a sign that she was succeeding, albeit in a way she hadn't foreseen and in a circumstance with which she wasn't completely comfortable. Unsurprisingly, she decided to come and watch, both to give me advice as needed and to make sure I didn't hurt myself.

I led Cassie to our round pen and set her loose. Just as Roy was learning to tell Rowdy to move at different speeds in either direction, I taught Cassie to follow my commands, using the flag and my voice to encourage her to do what I asked and dissuade her when she did something that I didn't ask her to do. It was a blistering hot summer day, so I had chosen my attire to beat the heat rather than for fashion: a red t-shirt, black basketball shorts, and my black cowboy boots. After all, Cassie only cared what I did, not how I looked. And I was counting on her not to buck me off, since the sandy footing of the round pen would have caused a severe road rash on my bare legs if I fell.

Eventually I put the halter back on Cassie and threw the saddle on her back. Most young horses get spooked when they first have a saddle put on. Horses see a different picture in each eye, and it frightens them when a saddle suddenly appears in their vision as it swings over their backs. But Cassie was used to me swinging over her, so a saddle was no problem. She stood quietly while I tightened the cinch.

I then turned her loose and sent her around the pen again, letting her get used to the feel of the saddle on her back while she moved. She handled it easily, not bucking in fright like many youngsters do. Once

Mom and I were satisfied with her demeanor, I asked her to stop. When she did, I put the rope halter back on, threw the lead rope around Cassie's neck, and tied the loose end under her chin to create reins without using a bit and bridle. I then put my foot in the stirrup and swung into the saddle for the first time.

At first, Cassie was nervous about moving forward while I was perched atop the creaking saddle, but rather than prancing, she stood quietly, not comprehending the command to move forward from the pressure of my legs against her sides. I asked her to bend her neck to either side, which she did at the lightest touch of the reins, but no amount of coaxing or urging could get her to take a step forward. Finally, Mom stepped into the center of the ring and picked up the training flag. She flicked it to coincide with my legs tapping against Cassie's sides, helping her to associate the unknown command of leg pressure to the already-learned command to move forward when directed by the flag. Cassie circled the pen at a walk, following my direction as I asked her to turn, reverse direction, and stop.

At last, heart pounding in excitement, I urged Cassie to move faster, speeding up first into a foxtrot then a canter. Cassie obeyed, flying around the circle as a smile broke across my face. Together we had managed to navigate the first steps to becoming an unbreakable team of horse and rider. I couldn't help but feel vindicated for my assertion that Cassie was the right horse for me.

Like Roy, I had watched *The Noble Horse* in order to learn more about round pen training. The thing that caught my attention, however, was not in the round pen; it was the fact that Bryan Neubert spent two days working with a horse in the round pen and arena, both on the ground and on its back, and on the third day, he rode it outside, even if it was a wild horse that had never been touched before. And even though I was far from being as skilled as the world-class trainer, my filly was gentle and sweet, and I had been training her for her entire life. I would not be outdone.

On the second day of Cassie's official training, I rode her in the arena after I finished in the round pen, and on the third day, ignoring Mom's protests, I opened the gate of the arena and rode Cassie out of the safe confines of the sandy oval. The mile-long loop around our property was a short ride for a trail horse, but it was a huge milestone in the foundation of the bond of trust between the gangly filly and girl.

A week after I started riding Cassie, I entered the seventh grade. Summers in the town of Winters are brutally hot, so I avoided the blazing sun by getting up an hour early to ride Cassie before school. I wanted to spend as much time on Cassie before Mom sent her to Neubert, the master himself, to solidify the basics and teach her things that I didn't know how to do yet, such as side-passing, pivoting, and getting desensitized to things we would encounter on the trail, including stream crossings and wildlife encounters. After an early morning ride on Cassie, I went to school with Brian.

While Brian and I were in school, Mom would pick Roy up and take him shopping if she had any errands to run. Taking Roy to Costco, Mom's most frequented store, usually added about an hour to the trip. Roy followed Mom around as she pushed her cart up and down the aisles, stocking up on all the necessities and food that seemed to get used up immediately, despite being bought in bulk. Roy would trail behind at his slow shuffle, causing Mom to subconsciously slow from her normal power walk to allow him to catch up. Yet no matter how slow she went, Roy always straggled by a couple feet. Once she realized what he was doing, she pointed it out and joked, "Roy, you'd be the perfect trail horse. We have to teach our horses to stay the same distance behind us while we're leading them." Roy laughed, but nothing Mom said could make him walk next to her, so instead she went at her normal pace and made poor Roy hustle to keep up.

Mom occasionally suggested that Roy sit in the food court and have a blue pop while she shopped, but Roy refused. Cell phones weren't common yet, so Roy would have no way of getting ahold of either Mom or Steve if something happened and he couldn't find Mom in the huge store. He had anxieties about being accidentally left behind, so Mom simply scheduled extra time whenever she took Roy shopping.

Mom also decided to start taking steps to help Roy become more independent. As a teenager, Mom had spent a semester in West Berlin as a foreign exchange student when the Berlin Wall was still in place. During one holiday, she and the two daughters of her host family took a trip throughout Europe, traveling alone on the railway system for almost two weeks. What made an impression upon Mom wasn't the exotic places she saw or the people she met, but rather the freedom that she and the two girls had to travel by themselves. When she began raising Brian and me, those memories of her months in Europe starkly contrasted what she saw in the generation of "helicopter parents" currently inundating the United States.

As Mom grew closer to Roy, she resolved to help him step out of his comfort zone and become more independent. Glenys had done her best to raise her son throughout the difficulties he faced, but Roy was still heavily reliant on others. He had learned early on that when something was difficult or made him feel uneasy, he could ask someone else to do it for him and therefore avoid the situation. When Mom started taking Roy shopping, she soon implemented a plan for making him more self-sufficient. It started out small—"Go get a loaf of bread and then meet me in the next aisle"—since Roy was uncomfortable with getting out of Mom's sight. Each successful task was then rewarded by a hug and praise. The little steps toward greater independence had an impact on Roy's round pen training as well. Rather than stepping in and "rescuing" Roy when he struggled, Mom instead taught him the tools he needed so that he could rescue himself.

If Mom had taken Roy shopping that day, he sat in the front seat when the diesel Suburban rumbled to a halt in the pick-up area of the middle school. Brian, who usually sat in the front due to his brotherly habits of pulling my hair or poking me if he was behind or next to me in the car, was relegated to the back seat with me. Fortunately for me, he was finally old enough to want to appear cool and mature in front of adults other than our parents, so he was usually able to restrain the impulse to torment me on the fifteen-minute ride back home.

Once at Red Tail Farm, Roy would practice his round pen training techniques with Rowdy after he'd gotten the chance to sit and enjoy an ice-cold pop or a steaming cup of coffee, depending on the weather. In the round pen, Roy listened to Mom and followed her directions, and in turn Rowdy listened to Roy and followed his directions. As the months went on, a bond began to form between Roy and Rowdy.

The people-shy, maltreated horse found a kindred spirit in the quiet voice and gentle hands of Roy, who knew what it felt like to be abused and neglected. He understood Rowdy's pain in a way that few could understand. Looking at Rowdy was seeing a vision of his past, recollecting the mistrust of other humans that he himself had once known. Roy had found healing and peace through his faith in God, and his ability to forgive those who mistreated him allowed him to move past the memories of pain and rejection. Though Roy is not an outspoken evangelist, the love inside him is evident to anyone who meets him, whether two-legged or four.

In the round pen, Rowdy taught Roy the finer techniques of command through body language by his obedience to subtle movements, and in return, Roy imparted to Rowdy one of the most critical lessons Roy had learned in his six decades: how to trust a human being. When Rowdy made a mistake, Roy didn't raise his hands and voice in anger; likewise, when Roy erred, the horse didn't ridicule and belittle him. Tears of frustration were occasionally shed on Roy's part, but together the two scarred souls formed an enigmatic bond as they taught and strengthened one another.

One of the most significant moments in their training came one day as Roy and Rowdy stood in the center of the round pen. As he always did, Rowdy stood stiffly while Roy scratched his neck; the horse's head was high in the air, alert for danger and ready to run if necessary. But as Roy continued to pet him, Rowdy began to lose his fear. He lowered his head with a sigh of contentment as he relaxed under Roy's gentle ministrations, unwinding from the constant ready-to-flee position that he normally held around people.

From that moment, it wasn't too long before Roy mastered what can be one of the most rewarding aspects of round pen training: having the horse follow without a halter or lead rope. In order to accomplish this, the trainer must teach the horse that he is the horse's friend, and that the best place for the horse to be is with the trainer. To the amateur eye, it may seem that the trainer is closer to being the horse's enemy than his friend. After all, it is the trainer who is making the horse run around in circles, with little effort on his own part since he is commanding the horse from the center of the ring, and therefore not having to move very much, while the horse must circumnavigate the entire pen. But when the trainer backs up to ask the horse to stop, the horse is expected to turn toward the trainer and walk to the center of the ring.

This doesn't happen on the first try. The trainer builds up to this point with baby steps; for example, to start, the horse may just turn his head toward the middle of the pen. Later, he turns his whole body; next, he takes a few steps, until, finally, he walks all the way to the center. The trainer encourages this by giving the horse the reward of resting when he does the right thing and keeps his focus on the trainer when he is stopped. If the horse does something other than what the trainer wants—such as turning his body away from the trainer to look out of the round pen at the horses in the barn—the trainer makes the horse move his feet and continue around the ring.

Horses may not be the geniuses of the animal kingdom, but they are smart enough that it usually doesn't take them too long to figure out that the best place for them to be is next to the trainer. After all, when they are with the trainer, they don't have to work, and, as a bonus, the trainer pets and scratches them. It gets to the point that the horse will follow the trainer when he moves, knowing that if he doesn't stay within a couple of feet of the trainer, he will have to work hard again.

Roy finally achieved that level of rapport with Rowdy in the spring of 2002, about a year after he first practiced in his living room while watching the Neubert training video. Once Roy figured it out, it was rather comical to watch the two of them in the round pen; Roy would turn sharply to double back on Rowdy and alternately speed up and slow down, doing his best to "lose" him. Rowdy was dogged in his pursuit of

Roy, pivoting and side-passing to keep behind Roy as the man quickly turned toward Rowdy's flanks.

The movements of Roy and Rowdy had transformed from a disjointed series of actions and reactions to a harmonious dance, with two partners moving together around a sand ballroom. Although they never touched while in motion, Rowdy followed Roy's lead like a graceful dancer as Roy began to finally master the art of working in a round pen.

Chapter 7
Selling the Horses

IN THE FALL of 2001, the same time that I was first beginning to ride Cassie, Mom decided to stop breeding horses and sell her broodmares. Managing a herd of over thirty horses was taking too much time away from her husband and son (although all the horses meant plenty of mother-daughter time). That decision led to several tough choices: which horses would go, and which would be kept as riding mounts? A few answers were clear: Cassie, Damien, and Rowdy were staying at Red Tail Farm.

Duke was staying as well, though his days as a stallion were numbered. Mom took Bryan Neubert's advice, which he had given her years earlier: "If you stop breeding horses, either sell Duke for a lot of money, or geld him and ride him." Mom decided to follow the latter option. The mares were already pregnant, due to give birth in the spring of 2002. Those were destined to be his last babies.

Mom chose to start selling the mares immediately, since pregnant broodmares can sell for more money than barren ones, and foals can be difficult to sell. After all, most buyers want a horse old enough to ride because they don't want to have to wait for it to grow up. The only mare that Mom wanted to keep was Cloud's Rain Dance, a beautiful little gray horse that had been the first live foal born on the ranch.

When Mom decided to sell all the mares, she called John Segale, offering him first pick. The year before, John had bought Cassie's older brother, a palomino colt named Yolo Gold. At that time, he asked Mom to notify him if she ever decided to sell her mares, since he was interested in buying one. The same afternoon that Mom told him the mares were for sale, John and his wife, Mary Lou, came over with their truck and trailer and looked at the small band of mares in their paddock.

"The only one not for sale is Rain Dance, the little gray mare," Mom said.

John walked among the mares, examining their conformation. "I really like the gray one," he finally confessed.

"John!" Mary Lou scolded, embarrassed. "That one isn't for sale."

I was perched on top of the fence, happily slurping on an ice cream bar, watching the proceedings as John looked over the mares once again. I wanted to see which one would be going to a new home.

"Okay, I guess I'll take the chestnut then," John said.

I froze. There were two chestnut mares in the group, Tomboy and DeeDee. But it wasn't Tomboy that John was pointing toward.

It was DeeDee, my favorite mare and the mother of Cassie and Yolo Gold. She was so sweet and gentle that I could jump on her bareback with only a halter and ride her around the barn, even though her only training had been years earlier and had only lasted for thirty days. I had known that she was for sale, but it had never crossed my mind that she might be the first to go.

"Not DeeDee!" My voice broke as tears streamed down my face. I hastily wiped my cheeks, averting my eyes as the three adults looked at me in surprise; I was normally a tomboy, and I never cried in public.

"You can buy Rain Dance," Mom said immediately. The sacrifice Mom was making for me didn't register. All I knew was that I got to keep DeeDee for a little while longer.

"Deal," John said. He and Mary Lou paid Mom and then loaded Rain Dance in their trailer and took her away. Mom was stoic and didn't cry when her beloved mare left Red Tail Farm. Her daughter's happiness was more important than keeping a horse, even Rain Dance.

The next spring, DeeDee gave birth to her final foal at Red Tail Farm. Like his sire, Magic Duke, the colt was black with no white markings, so Mom registered his name as Magic's Carbon Copy.

"What are we supposed to call him?" I asked. Many of our foals had the word magic in their names, including Magic Moment, Magic Attitude, Magical Marcella, Magical Annie, and Sweet Magic. Therefore, we couldn't just call the colt "Magic," and "Carbon Copy" didn't exactly roll off the tongue.

"Well, you think of a nickname for him," Mom said. "We are going to keep him."

The colt had the same sweet nature as Cassie and DeeDee, as well as legs that seemed like they would never end. From his first wobbly step, it was easy to foresee his destiny as a gentle giant, although none of us knew then that the gangly colt would have a major role to play in Roy's future.

As an avid fan of *The Lord of the Rings,* I decided to give the black colt an elvish name. After a long time searching through an English-Elvish dictionary, I settled on a translation of his description—Halla Vorn Rokko, or Tall Black Horse. And so, Rokko was named.

Since we were selling most of our herd, Grandma Lulu decided she should take one of our young horses as a future replacement for her aging mare. During one of Grandma's visits to Red Tail Farm, she went out to the barn to look at the band of weanlings. She wasn't sure which one she wanted, since to her all the black foals looked nearly identical, but as she watched them, the decision was practically made for her. One of the many barn cats decided to climb up the leg of one of the fillies, Angelita. Instead of kicking the cat or running away, Angelita calmly picked up her leg and gently shook the cat off. Grandma knew that was the horse for her: calm and gentle. Ironically, she decided to call the filly Kick, because, "She's a kick in the pants."

Once Grandma had chosen her new horse, we set a date for the filly to make the thousand-mile trailer ride back to Colorado. To save Grandma and Grandpa from having to do too much driving, Mom decided to haul Kick over the Sierra Nevada Mountains to Reno, where the horse would be transferred to Grandma and Grandpa's trailer. Mom was worried about her parents having to load and unload a yearling—even starting from Reno, the drive was long enough to warrant an overnight stay in Elko,

Nevada, with Kick spending the night at the fairgrounds—so in the manner of the military, I was "voluntold" to serve as horse handler for the trip.

Meeting in Reno served an ulterior purpose as well. The Bureau of Land Management (BLM) was holding an adoption clinic for Mustangs, and Bryan Neubert was hired by the BLM to lead clinics that demonstrated to new Mustang owners how to handle and train their new mounts.

Mom made the most of the opportunity and invited Roy, Steve, and their good friend Al Roth, a former Thoroughbred jockey, to come to Reno and watch Neubert at work. Roy was thrilled to finally see Neubert in person, the man in whose footsteps he had literally followed as he watched the tape of Neubert training and mimed his movements and body language.

When we arrived at the Reno fairgrounds midmorning, we pulled into the far end of the parking lot, where no cars were parked save Grandma and Grandpa's silver Dodge Ram truck, hooked to their small trailer. Mom parked next to them, and after short pleasantries, I unloaded Kick from our trailer. She barely had a chance to glance around before it was back into a metal box for her, as I immediately loaded her into the other trailer.

My grandparents and I still had another three hundred miles to drive before we reached our overnight stay in Elko, and we wanted to get Kick settled in at the fairgrounds before it was dark, so shortly after we transferred Kick, we hit the road again.

As my grandparents and I pulled out of the parking lot on our way to Colorado, Mom, Roy, Steve, and Al headed inside to watch Neubert's BLM Mustang clinic. It was held in a huge building, large enough to hold an arena and some small stands for spectators. They settled down to watch as Neubert demonstrated the fundamentals of starting a Mustang. Afterward, the four of them went down to the arena, and Mom introduced them to Neubert.

Bryan Neubert was every inch what one imagines when the word "cowboy" comes to mind. Spurs softly clinked on the heels of his boots, which were adorned with dust and grit rather than oil and polish. His jeans were protected by well-worn leather chinks with fringe that swung with each stride. A long-sleeved plaid shirt was tucked in, revealing a sturdy leather belt fastened by a large silver buckle. An off-white western hat sat on his head, covering most of his short-cropped silvering hair and shading his piercing blue eyes. Those eyes held kindness that extended to Roy when they met and continues to this day.

Roy was ecstatic to meet Neubert, who had already heard about Roy's progress in the round pen from phone calls from Mom. He encouraged Roy to continue his good work and gave him his phone number so that Roy could call him with any questions—or just to chat. The two men didn't get a long time to talk that day, but their friendship continued through the telephone, and it wouldn't be the last time they would cross paths.

Chapter 8
Entering the Spotlight

ON SATURDAY, APRIL 28, 2002, Roy returned to the Winters Youth Day Parade. While before he had ridden in the back of a green Mustang, this time he was to ride on the back of a gold Fox Trotter. John Segale offered to let Roy ride his horse, Domo, through the parade. Domo was actually Yolo Gold, whom John had renamed to the Japanese word for "much," shortened from the phrase "Domo arigato," which means "thank you very much." Domo had been a present from John's wife, Mary Lou. Roy was eager to ride the palomino gelding in the parade, so early Saturday morning, John trailered his horse to Winters.

I played trumpet in the Winters Middle School Band, and we were scheduled to march through the parade, blaring out "Another One Bites the Dust," which we had spent the prior month playing and memorizing. We had also spent time practicing our marching skills; since it would be distracting to other classes to march around the school, we instead marched through the neighborhood surrounding the school during our hour-long band period, no doubt causing many of the local residents to seriously regret their choice of real estate.

Not willing to be left out of the festivities, Mom decided to enter the parade as well, riding Damien as a solo horse entry. We parked in a large, empty field on the outskirts of town, which was set aside as horse trailer parking for all the equine entries, which ranged from a team of miniature mules pulling a tiny wagon to the dancing stallions of a mariachi band. Dad drove separately in his small car so that he could pick up Roy on the way and then leave immediately after the parade, skipping the festivities of Youth Day in the park afterward.

I hopped out of the Suburban and went in search of the band. It was still a few hours before the start of the parade, but we were required to assemble early for judging, although since we were the only middle school band in the parade, we were guaranteed the trophy just for showing up on time. It wasn't difficult to find the band, a motley assembly of youths in black t-shirts and jeans, blasting and banging their various instruments to alleviate the boredom of waiting. I checked in with the band teacher and then joined a few of my fellow brass players in a high spirited rendition of the *Star Wars* theme song.

Back at the trailers, Mom and John got Damien and Domo ready for the parade, brushing their manes and tails, cleaning the last few persistent spots of dirt, and lacquering their hooves with hoof polish. At the last minute, just before the judging was finished, Dad and John helped Roy climb a mounting block and then heaved him into Domo's saddle.

After Roy and Domo had been inspected by the parade judge, John led them down the side streets to the lineup area for equestrian entries. As they waited for the commencement of the parade, Mom learned that she would be the last horse in the parade, directly in front of one of the girls from my 4-H horse club, Holly, who was the parade's "pooper scooper" that year. Usually, there were a few teams signed up as pooper scoopers, each vying for a fifty-dollar cash prize. That year, however, Holly was the only person willing to be a pooper scooper, which guaranteed her the money but also meant she had to clean up after every single horse in the parade, a daunting task considering the number of horses. Not only were there dozens of horses entered in the parade, but horses empty their bowels when they're nervous, and the loud noises and unfamiliar sights in parades are nerve-wracking for them.

John and Roy were several spots ahead of Mom in the parade, but in the waiting lineup it wasn't too important to stay in the exact parade order. Instead of standing on the pavement underneath the steadily warming sun, John halted Domo in the shade of a tree at the edge of the park in order to keep Roy as comfortable as possible. Dad waited nearby, bottles of water in hand as he acted as attendant for Roy, John, and Mom. I took advantage of the long wait to ditch the band for a moment and see the equestrians, giving Roy a pat on the leg since he was too high for his customary hug. Perched on top of the gold and white gelding, Roy looked as if his face would split in two, the king of the town on his royal steed.

Before the parade started, the bottles of water that Dad generously handed out began to take effect, and Roy needed to get out of the saddle. Fortunately, John and Dad were both big men, and they were able to slow Roy's descent and keep him from falling as he slid down the tall horse's side to the ground. Once Roy was ready to remount, a nearby picnic table in the park was utilized as a mounting block, and Roy was able to clamber back into the saddle just in time.

The interminable wait finally ended, and the colorful, writhing serpent of the parade began slithering down Main Street. The rat-a-tat of snare drums set the beat of the march, and the semi-ordered rows of the band moved, legs more or less in unison as we progressed down the street. When we crossed Fourth Street, the official starting line of the parade, the signal was given and we lifted our instruments, blasting out the opening notes of "Another One Bites the Dust," competing with the wailing of firetruck sirens, the jauntily blaring brass instruments of the mariachi bands, and the obnoxious blowing of plastic vuvuzelas by the crowd.

When their turn finally came, John led Domo out onto the street, Roy holding the saddle horn with one hand, waving to the crowd with the other. As they had during his first appearance in the parade, the crowd responded loudly to Roy, calling to him by name, waving furiously, and blowing their vuvuzelas even more passionately.

But not everyone in the crowd was as kind to all the entrants. Several groups back from Roy was Mom on Damien, followed by Holly, who struggled to clean up after the dozens of horses that had already traversed the route. She dragged her wheelbarrow down the street, stopping to shovel up the piles of manure scattered on the pavement. It took less than a block for her to fall behind, the gap widening between her and Damien as the parade participants were forced to slow to a crawl behind her.

"Hurry up!" A man in the crowd jeered. "What are you, stupid?" Even in a small, peaceful town like Winters it is impossible to fully escape the mean-spirited souls who seek to degrade and humiliate. "What the hell is your problem, girl?" Vehicles directly behind Holly in the parade honked their horns.

Mom glanced back to see what was taking Holly so long just in time to see her sob. Holly was frozen in fear and shame, and she hid her eyes behind her hands as the traffic horns blared. Immediately Mom turned Damien, trotted back down the parade route to where Holly stood, and swung to the ground.

"It's okay, Holly," Mom said, giving her a hug. "Here, you take Damien and lead him."

She handed Damien's reins to the embarrassed girl, relieving Holly of her shovel at the same time. They continued down the parade route, slowly catching up to the rest of the horses, Holly leading Damien while Mom scooped the manure. They finished the parade in that manner, Mom cleaning, Holly leading, and Damien happily prancing down the street, arching his neck and showing off for his admirers on the sidewalk.

Chapter 9
It's Showtime

ONE OF THE many challenges of running a horse-breeding ranch is advertisement, and one of the ways Mom solved this problem and marketed our horses was by exhibiting them in horse shows. Two shows for both Missouri Fox Trotters and Tennessee Walkers, a similar gaited breed, were held annually at Ranchotel in Vacaville. Mom would sometimes bring a young horse that she was trying to sell and ride it in the shows, and once I began riding Cassie, I started competing with her as well. While Cassie was definitely not for sale, she was still good advertisement for the ranch because she exhibited the quality of horses being produced at Red Tail Farm.

I had recently stopped showing Damien at 4-H horse shows. At the last one I entered, I lost the Dollar Bill Ride, which was the only thing that kept me coming back to them. If I had lost the competition fairly, I would not have quit, but I was cheated out of my prize money. The judge called a halt to the proceedings when there was only one senior rider left, ignoring the fact that both Sarah and I, both beginners, still retained our dollars. When Sarah and I protested, we were told that we were disqualified because we didn't canter, despite the fact that the rules forbade us to canter, and the judge herself had instructed us during the event: "Juniors and seniors, move up to a canter. Beginners, continue to trot."

After the show, Mom and Sarah's mother called and wrote to complain about the unethical results. The only response they received was, "We'll send your girls' dollars back to them."

Lacking both an apology and my winnings, I quit. It wasn't worth it to lose every competition of the day because I had a gaited horse if the authorities were also going to cheat me out of my single win. Besides, it was time to move on to a younger horse, Cassie, and a greater showing challenge—the largest equine exposition in North America.

Although Red Tail Farm was located in rural farmlands, every June brought with it the advertisement opportunity of a lifetime. The Western States Horse Expo was held annually at the Cal Expo Fairgrounds in Sacramento, a mere hour's drive from the ranch. Part of the numerous and comprehensive events during the three-day weekend event was a "breed showcase," which features representatives of the broad spectrum of horse breeds, from the adorable American Miniature Horse to the majestic Friesian. Fortunately for us, the Pacific Coast Fox Trotter Association had a strong presence at the Horse Expo at the time.

John Segale was a more active member of the Pacific Coast Fox Trotter Association and had participated in the Horse Expo before. He gave Mom the lowdown on the ins and outs of the Horse Expo, and in early June we loaded Rowdy and Cassie—both sparkling clean from baths, their whiskers and bridle-paths neatly trimmed—into the trailer for a trip to the cacophonous hodgepodge that is the Horse Expo.

We pulled around to the back of the sprawling fairgrounds, following the line of horse trailers, which came in as many different shapes and sizes as their occupants. The horse barns were simple structures, two rows of box stalls lined up and connected back to back, so that spectators could walk up and down each side to view the occupants within. There were three such barns bordering a large outdoor rectangular arena, two on the long side of the arena with the gate in between, and one on the short side of the arena, behind the announcer's box. Shaded grandstands for the spectators lined the other long side of the arena.

The horse stalls were already assigned and grouped based on breed, so before we unloaded our horses, we went in search of our designated stalls. John and his son, Derek, had already arrived and unloaded their horses, which we easily found due to the signs hanging from their stalls, indicating each horse's name, breed, and owner. John brought Domo, and Derek had his Fox Trotter, a chestnut sabino mare named Pippi. The stalls next to Domo and Pippi were empty, so we spread out shavings, filled up water buckets, and unloaded our horses into them.

On Cassie's stall, I hung a sign that read: "Delightful Cassie/Missouri Fox Trotter/Owner Lauren Filarsky." One of my hobbies at the time was wood burning, and the week before I had burned the letters into a wooden plaque for the Expo.

Roy was visiting while I worked on it and asked what I was doing.

"Nothing much," I replied. "But if you want, I have a lollipop you can have." I brandished the wood-burning tool, a thin instrument with a plastic handle and metal rod about the size of a pencil, which was red-hot and had a decorative tip attached. Smoke curled up from where a sliver of wood had stuck to it. "It might be a little hot, though."

Roy took a closer look at what I was doing and laughed uproariously. "It might be a little hot," he gasped. "Hehehehe." I smiled and went back to burning the letters that I had painstakingly traced on the board, smoke curling up from the blackened wood.

It was with a touch of pride that I hung my new sign from Cassie's pen, looping a brass chain I had attached to the board through the wire mesh of the stall gate. Cassie walked restlessly within, sniffing and pawing at the unfamiliar shavings and peering out at the activity nearby. The door to the stall was divided into a top and bottom section, so that when the top section was open, the occupant could stick its head out and look around. Mom told me to leave it closed, to prevent anyone from doing anything stupid, like sticking their fingers in her mouth, a surprisingly common occurrence when non-equestrians get the opportunity to see a horse close up.

In the stall next to Cassie was Rowdy, who stood stiffly in the back, staying as far from everyone as possible. He had never been to a show before, let alone an event as busy as the Expo. We threw some hay to both horses; Cassie immediately started eating, but Rowdy ignored the pile in his stall. His eyes were wide and worried, his ears flicking nervously at the different sounds.

We left the horses alone to settle in, and I took a quick look at the other Fox Trotters that were in the adjacent stalls. I gave Domo a quick pat; I had an affinity for him because he was Cassie's full brother. Domo wasn't the only palomino Fox Trotter present, and he paled in comparison to the other, a majestic stallion named Tornado's Sawdust. Both palominos had white manes and tails, but where Domo's coat was a light yellow, Sawdust's was a rich dark gold that gleamed metallically in the sunlight.

Many horses that are a spectacular color like Sawdust have poor conformation, since the breeder focused predominantly on color, rather than on other important qualities. That was not the case with Sawdust. He was built well, had a quiet disposition, and foxtrotted smoothly. I fell in love with his beautiful color, and wished that one day I'd have a horse like him. Ten years later, when I was looking for a stallion to breed with Cassie, I discovered one of Sawdust's sons, who was just as magnificent as his sire, both in color, personality, and smooth gait. A year later, Cassie gave birth to Moonlight Delight, a beautiful palomino filly with the same metallically golden coat as her sire and grandsire, the fulfillment of my decade-long dream.

But that year at the Horse Expo, I had no idea that one day my dream would be fulfilled. Instead I pushed my fantasy to the back of my mind and focused on having fun and doing my best in the breed demonstration.

The Horse Expo didn't open until the next day, Friday, so we had the entire afternoon to get our horses settled in and unload our tack and clothes for the weekend. Slightly set apart from the three exhibitioners' barns was a fourth barn. The stalls in that barn were set aside as makeshift tack and dressing rooms for the equestrians. John had already procured one for use by everyone with Fox Trotters, where we placed the myriad of necessary items for the next three days.

One of the hardest things about bringing a horse to the Expo, or to a regular horse show for that matter, is keeping clean. This applies to not only the horse, who by a classic application of Murphy's Law always seems to find a large pile of manure or mud pit to roll in as soon as it is bathed, but to the rider, who must have spotless clothing. Keeping the clothes clean is made even more difficult by the fact that Mom decided that she and I should wear dressy shirts that were white, a color that contains magnetic properties to attract all the dirt and colorful liquids in a fifteen-foot diameter. So naturally our clothes were protected by a dust proof layer of plastic and wouldn't be donned until the last possible moment before the breed demonstration, after our horses were already tacked in their meticulously oiled and polished saddles and bridles.

By the time we had finished unloading, Rowdy still hadn't touched his hay. We decided to give him his privacy, since even at home he would refuse to eat if anyone was looking at him, and we went home to eat our own dinner.

I was barely able to sleep that night, excited about the upcoming Expo. It took forever for the sun to finally reappear, and when it did, it came with a vengeance. It was still marginally cool as Mom and I headed out toward Sacramento, but the sun was destined to flirt with triple digits the entire weekend.

Cassie nickered a greeting when she saw me approaching her stall. It would have been touching to know that she was happy to see me, except for the fact that her eyes were locked onto the flake of hay I was carrying toward her. I opened the top partition of the gate and tossed it in, then leaned into her stall so I could check her water bucket. Cassie had sucked off the top half during the night, so I dragged a hose over to refill it.

When Mom brought Rowdy his breakfast, she discovered that his hay from the night before was still untouched. Even more alarming, his water bucket was still filled to the brim. With the sweltering heat just a few hours away, it was dangerous for Rowdy to stop drinking. Mom decided to check on Rowdy throughout the day, to see if he would start eating and drinking once he got hungry and thirsty enough.

The schedule for the rest of the day was typical of horse shows and events: hurry up and wait. We arrived early in order to feed our horses, but it takes an average of two hours for a horse to finish eating. We weren't scheduled for a demonstration until late morning, so we had plenty of time after the horses finished eating to wait until we had to start getting ready. The fairgrounds were just starting to wake up, with retailers and food vendors arriving to open their booths and stands before the gates were unlocked and the morning crowd flooded in. We spent the time waiting with John and Derek, who had commandeered a small cabin-like shed with a shaded porch, where we reclined in folding camp chairs and watched the different horse people go about their morning chores.

When nine o'clock, the official opening time of the Horse Expo, finally rolled around, Derek and I decided to go look at the different vendors' booths. While Mom owned a cell phone—a blocky piece of equipment larger than most home phones these days—cell phones weren't common yet, and certainly weren't given to a pair of preteens. So John and Mom let Derek and me go, provided we followed the standard safety conditions: stay together, be careful, and, above all, be back in time to get ready for our demonstration. I pocketed my measly allowance money of a dollar a week that I'd been saving by default, since Mom usually forgot to pay Brian and me on time, and we'd get a handful of cash a few times a year.

The Western States Horse Expo vendors' booths contain everything a person can possibly imagine that relates to horses: tack, grooming supplies, feed, equestrian clothes, trailers, trucks, boots, even horse-themed art. Hawkers did everything in their power to convince shoppers of the miraculous abilities and unique qualities of their specific items and brands. Derek and I perused the warehouse-sized buildings that contained the staggering number of items for sale. I admired the beautifully-tooled leather gear, both for horse and rider, from breast collars and bridles for the horse, to boots and belts for riders.

Before long, it was time to return to the stables and get ready for our breed demonstration. As we walked back, Derek confided his plan to me.

"At the end of the demo, we all line up side-by-side, facing the stands," he said. "I'm going to put Pippi in the middle, and then stand up on her back and bow. I've been practicing."

"Cool. That sounds like fun," I said.

"Want to do it with me?"

I had never stood up on a horse's back before, but I wasn't about to be shown up by the only other person in our group that was my age.

"Sure," I replied.

"Okay, make sure you are at the end of one of the lines, then. At the end, they are going to turn down the middle two-by-two together and split at the center of the arena, so the leaders are on the ends and the last horses are next to each other in the middle."

By the time we arrived at the stable area, Dad and Roy were there. Dad had taken the day off work to come watch us, and he had picked up Roy along the way. I gave both of them hugs, and then I got Cassie out and started getting her ready for the demo.

Cassie sidestepped nervously at the hitching rail where she was tied while I brushed her glossy coat, cleaned debris from her feet, and combed her mane and tail, which were flecked with the wood shavings that comprised the bedding in her stall. I had scrubbed Cassie's white sock on her left rear leg to a gleaming ivory the day before, but overnight it had become soiled green with manure. I wiped the stain away as best as possible with a damp rag.

Cassie's head whipped from side to side, held high atop her arched chestnut neck as she tried to keep everything in her sight at once. Her eyes were wide, and her nostrils quivered with excitement. At the rail next to her, Rowdy stood as stiff and solid as a post. His ears were on a constant swivel, listening to the commotion and keeping track of every person who came within fifty feet of him. Cassie bumped into him a few times, but he didn't budge. He was a rock amidst a sea of chaos, with only his eyes betraying the terror within.

Once Cassie was ready, I went to the stall we were using as a tack room and changed, tucking my white shirt into ebony jeans that I cinched up with a black and silver leather belt. I wiped my boots off with a cloth, trying to make them as presentable as the rest of me. Most equestrians have a separate pair of boots that are specifically designated for shows, and therefore are kept safe and immaculate in a boot bag all the time, but I was at the age where I outgrew my shoes at about the same time they were finally broken in properly, and my regular black cowgirl boots were still new enough to be serviceable for a show.

As we mounted up and started riding in the small dirt warm-up area, Dad and Roy walked over to the stands to secure a spot in the shade to watch us ride. I kept Cassie close to Rowdy as we rode, her nose nearly brushing his tail. Young horses feel safer when they have a buddy to tailgate, since they don't have to be the first one to pass by scary objects. It can be unsafe to tailgate too closely to another horse, since many, especially mares, are prone to kicking when their personal space is invaded. But Rowdy had already proven his tolerance of tailgaters, even painful ones like Damien the butt biter.

At last, it was time. We lined up in a double column before the main arena gate, Derek and I side-by-side in the rear, flashing each other the mischievous smile of co-conspirators. The gates swung open and the announcer's voice crackled through the loudspeaker, reading the prearranged script that proclaimed the breed and described the different attributes of the Fox Trotters.

We entered at a foxtrot, the two lines splitting to circle the arena in opposite directions. A Fox Trotter in motion looks unusual in comparison to the typical horse, such as an Arabian or American Quarter horse, whose trot is a steady beat of one-two, one-two, one-two, the legs moving in paired harmony while the head and neck remain relatively level. By contrast, a Fox Trotter's legs move individually, tapping out a steady one-two-three-four while the head bobs rhythmically, often inducing the ears to flop forward and backward in beat with the head nod. It may look somewhat comical in comparison to the classic two-beat trot, but one only has to observe the rider to see the enormous benefits. When riding a horse that trots traditionally, the rider will be jarred and bounced with every stride, unless the rider posts, using their own legs to rise and fall with each bump. In contrast, the rider of a Fox Trotter has effortless comfort: the four-beat strides create a smooth, easy ride that has virtually no up-and-down bounce.

It was this smoothness that we demonstrated as we foxtrotted in simple patterns around the arena, following the line leaders. I ignored the crowd except to keep a smile affixed to my face, and instead concentrated on keeping proper formation spacing—one horse-length from Rowdy's tail—and on keeping Cassie at a foxtrot. She chomped nervously at the bit, prancing and fighting to speed up and catch up to Rowdy. I held her back, struggling to make my ride seem effortless. Because Cassie was young, she had a difficult time maintaining a foxtrot at the same speed as the older horses, breaking into a canter for a stride before I could rein her back.

As we made the final turn down the center, slowing to a walk, my heart struck a double-time beat against my rib cage. I clenched my fingers around the reins, sending up a quick prayer that pride wouldn't come before a fall—literally. I drew Cassie to a halt next to Derek and gave her neck one last pat to comfort her.

"Easy, Cass," I murmured, as next to me Derek began climbing on top of his saddle.

I took a deep breath, freed my legs from the stirrups and lifted my feet to the seat of the saddle, where I crouched for a brief second. Cassie's ears flicked back nervously, unsure about the shifting weight on her saddle.

"Whoa, girl," I said and, before I could change my mind, stood up. I kept a grip on my reins, which were stretched to the limit as I wavered unsteadily on the round, slick leather perch. Next to me, Derek removed his cowboy hat and bowed to the crowd. I wore a helmet, as always, so I couldn't take it off, but I was not to be outdone. I shakily bent at the waist in a quick bow. Derek and I gave one last wave to the crowd and then sat back down, unwilling to press our luck any further.

As I followed the line back out of the arena, relief washed through me. The demonstration had gone well and, more importantly, I hadn't fallen off and embarrassed myself in front of a few hundred people.

Once our horses were untacked and back in their stalls, Derek and I walked to the racetrack on the fairgrounds and watched a few harness races to pass the time. Unlike Thoroughbred racing, where the horses are ridden by a jockey, in harness racing the horses pull a small, two-wheeled cart called a sulky. Instead of galloping, the horses either trot or pace, depending on the breed and race. Trotting horses move their legs in a diagonal gait, with one front leg and the opposite rear leg moving at the same time, whereas pacing horses move in a lateral gait, with the front and rear legs on the same side moving in synchronization. Smooth-gaited horses, such as Fox Trotters and Paso Finos, were originally bred by cross-breeding different pacing and trotting breeds of horses.

After a few races, Derek and I returned to the stables and discovered that the day had a sour note: Rowdy was still refusing all forms of nourishment. By the late afternoon, Mom decided to take him home rather than risk his mental and physical health any further. The question that then arose was whether or not we would take Cassie home as well, since she would no longer have her buddy to follow during the exhibitions. John offered to watch out for me, letting Cassie follow Domo during the exhibition instead of Rowdy. We decided to test it out, and I got back on Cassie.

Horses do not understand the concept of having a sibling. Domo had been weaned a few months before Cassie was born, and since we kept our young horses segregated in different age groups, she had little to no interaction with her brother while he lived at Red Tail Farm. But Domo possessed the same quiet temperament that all of DeeDee's offspring had inherited, and he had an extra year of seasoning and experience under saddle. John and I rode around the stables for a little while. Cassie was nervous about all the commotion, but with the older horse to draw strength from, she did fine. We decided to leave Cassie at the Expo for the remainder of the weekend.

While I untacked Cassie, Roy offered to go catch Rowdy from his stall, since Mom was walking to the parking lot to bring over the Suburban and horse trailer. When I came back outside from the makeshift tack room after depositing my saddle, I saw that Roy was in trouble. Roy was using a standard web halter, rather than the rope halter he used when training Rowdy, and when he tried to put the halter on Rowdy, he accidentally twisted the strap that went behind Rowdy's ears, making it too short to reach the buckle.

Rowdy, scared by the crowds and noise, pushed close to Roy, seeking protection from one of the few people he trusted. But in the confines of the tiny stall, Rowdy had him trapped in the corner. He wasn't squishing Roy, but his close presence prevented Roy from being able to see that the halter was twisted as he struggled in vain to get it buckled, and there was no room for him to move away from the horse. Roy was slightly panicked by the claustrophobic feeling of a twelve-hundred-pound animal cornering him in a stall. He didn't realize that by holding onto the halter and continuing to futilely try to buckle it, he was preventing himself from being able to make Rowdy move away and stop crowding him.

"Help!" Roy called, but nobody else was in earshot to come to his rescue. I hurried over; I didn't run, because that would've only further spooked the already terrified horse. Instead I put my long legs to good use and stretched my stride to come to Roy's aid as soon as possible.

"Just a sec, Roy, you have the halter twisted," I said when I reached the stall. I swung open the gate and grabbed the offending strap and fixed the twist so Roy could buckle it properly. Once the halter was in place, Roy was able to ask Rowdy to back up and give him some space before he led the big horse outside.

It was late in the afternoon by the time we loaded Rowdy. I had already fed Cassie while Roy and I waited for Mom to bring the trailer around, so we left to go home for the evening. Dad took Roy in his car; that way, we didn't have to haul the trailer into town to drop Roy off at home.

As soon as Rowdy was at home in his stall (and he thought we weren't watching him), he took a long drink of water and finally settled into eating his hay, clearly relieved to be away from the noisy crowds.

Saturday at the Expo was even hotter than the previous day. The breed exhibition in the morning went as flawlessly as before, with Derek and me standing and bowing atop our horses at the end again. After we were finished and had cared for our mounts, Mom and John gave us money for admission into WaterWorld, which bordered the Expo. Instead of spending a miserable day sweltering in the heat, we splashed in the wave pool, floated with the current in the artificial river, and went rocketing down the wide variety of colorful multistory water slides.

The hours passed by all too quickly until it was time to return to the dry, dusty Expo and prepare for our afternoon show. After another uneventful demonstration, we fed our horses and left the fairgrounds in search of our own dinner. We didn't go home because the day wasn't over yet. On the schedule for that night was the Cavalcade of Horses, where all the different breeds being showcased at the Expo took turns entertaining the crowd in the main arena, which was more like a stadium, where the internationally known horse trainers held featured training demonstrations throughout the day.

After a quick bite to eat, we returned to the Expo to prepare our horses as the summer sun edged closer to the horizon. When we were ready, the Fox Trotters rode as a group across the fairgrounds to the stadium.

The scene at the horse entrance to the arena was one of barely contained chaos. The different groups lined up in order, cramming together in a paved parking lot area, which provided slippery footing and concrete trip-hazards for the horses. The entrance to the arena was also being used as an exit, so the horses that were finished had to somehow find room to squeeze out through the crowd while the following group tried to push their way into the spotlight. We were one of the last groups on the schedule, and the sun slipped below the horizon while we awaited our turn, reducing visibility to what could be seen in the flickers of halogen lights from the widespread lampposts. Horses snorted and pawed, dancing in place as they conveyed the excitement that spread throughout the group. I clutched Cassie's reins as she shifted restlessly at the back of the Fox Trotter group.

Directly behind me was a Percheron, hitched to a wagon that was driven by a man and a woman. The huge draft horse was scared, its dinner-plate-sized hooves banging against the asphalt as it pranced and side-passed, its white-rimmed fearful eyes searching for an escape from the bedlam.

"Get out of the way!" the man yelled at me. I turned Cassie, but there was no place for us to move in the tight-packed throng of horses.

"Move it!" the woman yelled.

"Oh, just run her over!" the man cried in frustration. I didn't hear his last words, because I finally spotted an escape in the sea of shifting animals and was focused on squeezing Cassie away from the nearly out-of-control draft horse. But Mom heard, helpless to do anything from where she watched on the edge of the moving expanse of horseflesh, and took note of who it was. The stables were small enough that she knew exactly who they were and where they kept their horse.

Fortunately, it was finally our turn in the arena. I followed Domo at the tail end of the Fox Trotter line as we gaited around the arena in a pattern of loops and figure eights. Because of the number of different exhibitors, the schedule was tight, and after only a few minutes foxtrotting beneath the glaring lights of the stadium, we were finished. The changed pace also meant that we didn't end in a stopped line in the center of the arena, but instead we trotted out the gate and made way for the next exhibitioner.

Back at the stables, I quickly took care of Cassie and put her away for the night. I was tired and happy that the long day was finally over.

"Are you ready to go?" Mom asked.

"Yes," I said.

"Okay, we need to do something first. I want to talk to those people with the draft horse that was behind you in the lineup," Mom said, and she grabbed my hand and marched around the corner to where the big Percheron was stabled. I was nervous; I didn't like confrontation, and I had no idea what Mom's plan was.

The owners of the Percheron had just put him in his stall. They were a husband and wife in their early thirties, still dressed formally from driving their wagon in the Cavalcade.

"Hello," Mom said pleasantly.

They greeted us in return, smiling now that the stress of the crazy night was over.

"My name is Cheryl Filarsky, and this is my daughter, Lauren," Mom said. We shook hands with them. "I just wanted to come over here and introduce you to my daughter. She is twelve years old and she was riding a three-year-old filly tonight." They looked confused, wondering why Mom was telling them this information, but smiled politely. In the poor light of the staging area earlier, they hadn't seen my face.

Mom's voice suddenly turned from sweet and soft to harder than granite. "I want you to look my little girl in the eye and know that she is the one you told your wife to run over tonight."

The color didn't drain out of their faces; it disappeared instantaneously. By that time, my eyes had welled up and spilled over with the rush of fear relived as Mom spoke.

"I am so sorry," the man instantly spluttered. "Our horse is just five and I was afraid we were going to lose control because he was scared. This is the biggest event we have ever done with him, and he couldn't handle all the commotion. I really didn't mean that; I don't know what came over me."

"That's okay," I mumbled.

"Would you like to meet him? He knows how to do tricks."

"Sure, I guess."

I walked into the stall with him to greet their young gelding. The average weight of a Percheron is nineteen hundred pounds, nearly twice that of a typical Fox Trotter, and while this one was still young, he was already nearing the end of his growth. His muscular gray body was so long that if he stood with his butt against one wall of his stall, he could easily stretch out his nose and touch the opposite wall.

Now that the horse was back in the stables where he felt safe, he was transformed from a barely controlled locomotive back to his inherent nature of gentle giant. Once I had petted him, the man lined the horse up diagonally in the stall and gave him a command. The great animal stretched out one front leg into the corner, bent the other, and lowered himself as far as he could in the confined area to bow for me. It was a tranquil ending to a dangerous evening.

The third and final day of the Expo was anticlimactic after the Cavalcade. We rode in a demonstration in the morning, Derek and I wandered the grounds and watched some more races in the afternoon, and, finally, once the Expo closed in the evening, we loaded Cassie in the trailer and drove home, relieved to leave the insanity behind.

Chapter 10
Did I Do All Right?

FOR ROY'S SIXTY-FOURTH birthday, the same summer we attended the Horse Expo for the first time, he didn't ask for presents. Instead, he asked for the opportunity to show his closest friends what he had been learning in the round pen. So Mom agreed to host the birthday bash at Red Tail Farm, and on the morning of July 6, 2002, the partygoers braved the pothole-ridden, county-maintained road to come to the ranch. Fortunately, the guest list was limited to a sliver of Roy's steadfast comrades, since even Mom's catering-grade chafing dishes wouldn't hold enough food for the entire town.

After the guests had all arrived, we walked out to the barn for the demonstration. Roy caught Rowdy and took him to the round pen. One of Roy's friends brought a camcorder, and he began to record as Roy led Rowdy through the gate. Mom had the microphone of a karaoke machine in hand so she could tell the small crowd what Roy was doing.

Roy stopped Rowdy in the center of the round pen, turning him so the crowd could see Rowdy's profile. Both man and horse were dressed for the occasion, Roy in brown slacks, a white Red Tail Farm polo shirt, and his ever-present baseball cap, this one from John Segale's Go Away Ranch. Rowdy was gleaming in the sun, wearing a bright red rope halter with a white lead rope. Roy lifted the lead rope high, wiggling it a bit, and Rowdy stretched out, moving his front feet forward while leaving his back feet still, until he was in a "parked out" position, with his hooves forming the corners of a long rectangle on the ground.

Once Roy had Rowdy parked out, he gave him a pat on the neck. Then, holding the rope in his left hand, he asked Rowdy to move by twirling the end of the rope with his right hand. Rowdy stepped forward and around Roy, so that Roy could walk over the spot where Rowdy had been standing. Rowdy followed Roy as Roy turned around to face him and started walking backward. When Roy changed direction and stepped forward toward Rowdy, this time with the lead rope in his right hand, Rowdy once again followed the rope and moved out of Roy's way, turning in a tight circle so that he was once again trailing Roy as Roy walked through Rowdy's footprints.

The exercise contained a few different vital horse-training aspects: Not only did it teach the horse to yield to the trainer and keep out of the trainer's space, it also taught the horse to yield softly to the pressure of the rope and to stay "hooked" on the trainer and maintain focus. Rowdy's abusive past made him quick to move out of Roy's way, but it also made it more difficult to build a desire to stay with his trainer. Having a lead rope on the horse made it easier to teach, somewhat akin to training wheels on a bicycle.

But months of working with Rowdy had forged such a strong bond between the maltreated horse and man that training wheels were no longer necessary. After a few more times of making Rowdy move out of his way in both directions, Roy stopped in the center of the round pen. Then Roy gave Rowdy a pat, took the halter off, and tossed it to the side. Rowdy stood still as Roy gave his neck a hug. Then Roy turned and walked away from the loose horse. Rowdy immediately followed, even stretching out his neck so he could sniff Roy's back as they walked.

It was nearly unbelievable to think that the placid gelding quietly following the man shuffling around the sandy enclosure was the same horse that used to tremble when touched. Roy sped up into his shuffling run, and Rowdy walked fast to keep up, then instantly halted when Roy stopped.

Roy turned and walked toward Rowdy's left flank. Rowdy pivoted, moving his hindquarters out of Roy's way and keeping his head following Roy. After taking a few steps forward, Roy again turned toward Rowdy's left flank. Rowdy followed again, but this time, instead of continuing straight after the horse turned, Roy reversed course and started trying to walk toward Rowdy's right flank. Since he was on Rowdy's left side, Rowdy's head was in the way. Rowdy turned away as Roy moved, bending his neck and pivoting to give Roy room, but not disconnecting himself from the invisible rope that kept him hooked to Roy.

When Roy and Rowdy stopped again, Roy rubbed Rowdy's face with his left hand, placing his right hand on Rowdy's neck and petting it, gently asking Rowdy to lower his head. Rowdy saw something outside of the round pen that startled him, so he quickly raised his head to look, his nose level with Roy's eyes. A few seconds later, he relaxed, slowly lowering his head until his bridle path—the area right behind a horse's ears where the hair is shaved so halters and bridles don't get tangled in the mane—was even with the bottom of Roy's chin. His body posture was the epitome of a completely relaxed horse.

Roy walked again, this time trying harder to lose his equine shadow. Rowdy followed his every move, refusing to be tricked whenever Roy suddenly changed direction. After a few minutes of follow the leader, Roy stopped and petted Rowdy again, then walked to the gate and got the training flag and a small bag of grain, which he hung over his shoulder.

Roy flicked the flag, and Rowdy started moving counterclockwise along the fence at a fast walk, speeding up to a foxtrot only when Roy asked. Getting Rowdy to walk in the round pen had been one of the hardest things for Roy to learn. Since Rowdy was so sensitive to body language, it didn't take much pressure to get him to speed up. Instead, it was difficult to be relaxed and have subtle enough commands that Rowdy would walk sedately, neither stopping nor hurrying up.

Roy then asked Rowdy to come to the center of the arena. Rowdy lowered his head and licked his lips as Roy petted him and gave him a handful of grain, then moved off as Roy sent him clockwise around the pen, this time at a slow walk. Roy spent the next several minutes working Rowdy, backing up a couple steps so Rowdy would turn into the center, then stepping forward to make Rowdy turn and go in the opposite direction. Rowdy foxtrotted and walked, taking his cues from the intensity of Roy's body language to know how fast he was supposed to move. Rowdy kept his head cocked toward Roy, watching and listening for Roy's different commands, then quietly executing them.

Roy finally put down the flag and asked Rowdy to return to the center of the round pen. Roy decided to scratch Rowdy's hindquarters, which was difficult considering that Rowdy was taught to follow Roy and move out of his way. It took a couple of tries, but after patiently moving his hands down Rowdy's body as he moved toward his rear end, Roy was finally able to scratch him without Rowdy moving.

Roy then walked away from Rowdy, who recognized the change and immediately started following. After a few more attempts at dodging Rowdy, Roy picked up the flag and carried it to the fence, where he handed it to me so I could put it away. Rowdy was still following him, since despite the fact Roy was carrying the flag, he didn't use it to tell Rowdy to go away. Roy returned to the center of the round pen, picked the halter up off the ground, and put it back on Rowdy.

Roy turned to the crowd and said, "Thank you."

"Is there anything you would like to add, Roy?" Mom asked into the microphone.

"Yeah." Roy walked over to the round pen gate, which was opened for him. "I would like to say something."

"Okay," Mom said, and she handed him the microphone.

Roy stood in the gateway, facing the guests, who sat on wooden benches we had brought over from our front porch for the training demonstration. Mom took Rowdy from him, and Roy stepped forward with the mike.

"You know, I enjoy my horse. But you know, it's important to work with a smart horse too. And this horse has been mistreated. And I was, long time ago, I was mistreated too. And I wanted to say thank you very much for all of you taking time and the energy to come over and be with me on my sixty-fourth birthday."

Everyone clapped. Roy started to hand the microphone back to Mom, but stopped. "Oh. Besides, thank you very much, Cheryl. You did a lot of work."

Roy traded the microphone for the lead rope as the guests clapped. He started leading Rowdy back to the barn, then turned and said, "Hey, if you want to come in the barn, I'll show you how to put a horse away."

"Okay, Roy, that's a good idea," Mom said.

All of us followed Roy into the barn, where he showed the guests how he led Rowdy into the stall, and then turned him around so that Rowdy's head was facing the gate before he took off the halter. That is the safe way to turn a horse loose, since the handler doesn't have to go past the horse's hindquarters to get to the gate, as sometimes horses like to buck and kick out in excitement when they are set free. Afterward, we all returned to the house for cake and presents.

The videotape of Roy's training demonstration turned out to be somewhat of a disappointment at first. The picture quality was decent, but there had been a slight but steady breeze that day, which meant the audio quality was terrible. A few snatches of commentary were discernible through the static-like roar, but it definitely didn't lend itself to easy and pleasant viewing. So Mom taped over the audio track, creating an informative monologue that allowed a non-equestrian viewer to know what both Roy and Rowdy were doing.

Roy was delighted with the resulting footage, and told everyone he saw about it, including the vice principal of Winters Middle School, who was an equestrian herself. She was interested in watching the tape, and Roy immediately gave her a copy. After seeing the film, she invited Roy to come speak at one of the middle school classes and share the video once school started again in the fall.

Two weeks after his birthday, Roy competed with Rowdy in the Paul Slaton Memorial Horse Show at the Ranchotel. It was a much smaller event than the Horse Expo, and it only lasted one day instead of three, so it was not too stressful for Rowdy to participate. Roy entered the halter class for Missouri Fox Trotter stallions and geldings. He led Rowdy around the arena with the other contestants, and then parked him out when they lined up in the center of the arena at the end of the class. Unfortunately for Roy, in halter classes the horse's conformation is the main judging point, and although Rowdy was calm and listened to Roy, he was built and moved more like a Tennessee Walker than a Missouri Fox Trotter. Still, Roy came away with a fifth-place ribbon, which he proudly hung on his wall at home.

Later in the day, Mom rode Rowdy in the country pleasure class, where the horse's behavior and smooth gait counts more than their conformation. Rowdy's gaits were buttery smooth, and Mom rode him into second place. I rode Cassie in the mares' foxtrotting class, and once again was the youngest competitor with the youngest horse, and once again I received a fourth-place ribbon.

The rest of the summer passed in a blur, and before I knew it, I was starting my eighth-grade year at Winters Middle School. I was dropped off at school extra early every morning, since Brian was beginning his high school career at Vacaville Christian and had to be dropped off after me, so I passed the time reading books as I waited for my friends to arrive. Soon I would have to decide if I wanted to go to Winters High School or willingly follow in my brother's footsteps to Vacaville Christian.

A few weeks into the school year, Mom started driving Roy to the middle school on Friday mornings to talk to one of the Prime Time classes, a thirty-minute homeroom period that occurred a couple hours after school started. During that class, teachers called roll, and then the students were generally free to pursue their own activities, such as homework that hadn't been finished the night before or perhaps a board game with their fellow classmates. I received permission from my Prime Time teacher to skip class on the days Roy came to school and instead go to his talk in a different class.

Mom bought Roy a new polo shirt for the occasion. It had his name, "Red Tail Farm," and a horse head with a streaming mane embroidered on the front left. Roy was nervous on the way to the classroom, needing constant reassurance that he was going to do well, despite his practice talking in front of crowds as a church deacon. After all, people in church are generally a welcoming crowd, whereas middle school students are often noted for their callousness and lack of mercy to those who are different.

I arrived at the classroom as the other students were filing inside. Mom and Roy were standing at the front of the room with the teacher, Roy visibly anxious but smiling and greeting the students who walked past him. Many of them knew him and said, "Hi, Roy," in return. I settled down at an empty desk in the back after I'd given Roy a hug.

The teacher quickly called roll and then said, "We have a special guest here today. For those of you who don't know, this is Roy Irwin. With him is Cheryl Filarsky. Roy has been learning to train horses at Mrs. Filarsky's ranch, and he has a video he would like to share with you." She clicked the play button on the VCR and switched off the lights.

We only watched about ten minutes of the video because the class was so short, but it was enough to give the students an idea of what round pen training was and what Roy had been doing with the horses.

"When I was your age, people said I couldn't do anything," he said after the video. His slight stutter, one of the main reasons he'd been written off as hopeless as a child, was more obvious due to nerves. "Kids used to make fun of me and call me a retard. I was institutionalized because they thought I was stupid. And you know what? They didn't even teach me to read or write or do numbers.

"They said I couldn't work, but I got a job at the Grosse Pointe Hunt Club. Cheryl, can you tell them what that is?"

"The Grosse Pointe Hunt Club is a boarding stable for horses near Detroit," Mom said. "The horses there are very expensive, and are used for jumping competitions. A lot of really wealthy people are members, like the Ford family. Roy worked there in his late twenties. Go ahead, Roy."

"The hunt club is back in Michigan, where I grew up," Roy continued. "There were a lot of horses there, and I brushed them and mucked out the stalls. I even got promoted to night watchman. Then my parents moved out to California, and we moved to Winters. I was really angry about the way people had treated me, and I got in a lot of fights. Then my baby brother, Steve, took me to church, and I met Jesus, and my life hasn't been the same ever since.

"I learned to read when I was fifty. Can you believe that? My teachers said I couldn't do it when I was younger, but I learned at the age of fifty.

"Then later on, I met Cheryl, and she took me to her ranch, and taught me how to train horses. I never knew I could do something like that. But I did it.

"So don't let other kids put you down and tell you that you can't do something. Because if I can do something at my old age, who knows what you can do. You can do anything. And be nice to one another, because words hurt. They hurt a lot more than you realize. Just remember to follow your dreams and do whatever you want."

When Roy finished, all the students applauded. Even the ones who had been disinterested when they heard the talk was going to be about horses were attentive, listening to Roy's every word. As they streamed out of the room to go to their next classes, Roy stood by the door and gave them either a hug or a handshake.

"Did I do all right?" he asked Mom once all the other students were gone.

"You did great, Roy," Mom replied.

Roy continued to come speak to a different Prime Time class every Friday. Mom bought him his own business cards, which bore his name, the title "Horse Trainer," and our ranch phone number, so Roy wouldn't be bothered by calls at home. Roy handed his business cards out like candy on Halloween to everyone he met, proud to have something to give others. He had a collection of business cards from other people and companies at home, part of a massive and unorganized collection of souvenirs and knickknacks that Steve dubbed "Irwin Relics." At last, Roy had his own "relics" to give away.

To help with his talks, Mom and Roy made an appointment with the pastor and an elder of Crossroads Christian Church to find out how much Roy could say about God in school. They informed Roy that it would be appropriate to include a statement that becoming a Christian changed his life, but not to proselytize to the students. Roy decided that working with horses was his way to gain admittance to school, but his goal was to say one sentence about how he changed when he was saved. For the rest of his talks, he spoke about loving each other, being tolerant of differences, and how important it is to follow your passion.

After every Friday presentation, Roy asked Mom the same question: "Did I do all right?" It was the same question he always asked when he was done with a session in the round pen with Rowdy. Roy's public speeches were getting stronger and flowing better as he practiced more, but he was still unsure of himself and didn't have confidence that he'd done a good job, a byproduct of being told the majority of his life that he was incapable of doing things by himself. So Mom always encouraged him and gave him a little constructive criticism to make his talks better, although not so much that he was discouraged.

At the end of the school year, the Winters Joint Unified School District invited Roy to a board meeting, where they presented him with an award for his uplifting work in the classroom. With a solid year of giving speeches every Friday under his belt, Roy set his sights on expanding his territory and giving talks at schools in neighboring towns.

Chapter 11
I Did Good

THE MORNING OF Saturday, April 26, 2003, dawned on the sixty-seventh annual Winters Youth Day Parade, and it once again saw the return of Roy Irwin to the parade route. Although Roy had enjoyed riding Domo in the previous year's parade, he was now an experienced enough horseman that he didn't want to be subjugated to being led on horseback. Instead, Roy was the leader. While I marched the streets with the Winters band for the last time, since I had decided to switch schools and attend VCS in the fall, Roy walked with Rowdy down the parade route.

About every hundred feet, Roy and Rowdy would stop; even though the parade wasn't very long, it moved at a slow crawl, held up as each entrant was announced in front of two judging stands. At each halt, Roy asked Rowdy to park out and pose for the crowd. Despite being nervous about the packed crowds on the sidewalks, Rowdy complied, trusting Roy to keep him safe from harm as he stretched out in a vulnerable position that would prevent him from being able to react quickly to danger. Roy would pat Rowdy's stiff chestnut neck, and Rowdy would dip his head slightly, nuzzling Roy in affection, before the pair continued down the street, only to stop and repeat the process once more a short while later.

Three weeks after the parade, the horse show season began for the Pacific Coast Fox Trotter Association. The commencement of the season marked the end of an era, for Roy and I were returning to the show ring at Ranchotel for the last time. Instead of competing with Cassie, I brought Duke, who had recently been gelded and was destined to be Rowdy's replacement as Mom's go-to riding mount. We no longer were in need of advertising the ranch, since the greatly reduced herd only contained horses we planned on keeping, but the show afforded an opportunity for exposing Duke to a new environment, since he had led a rather reclusive and sheltered life as a breeding stud; he had not left Red Tail Farm from the moment he arrived until after he was gelded over five years later. Mom planned on taking Duke to the Horse Expo that summer, and we decided to see how he did in the smaller and less hectic show first. Mom asked me to handle Duke in the show, since she preferred to spend the day as a one-woman cheerleading squad for Roy and me.

Although it was only mid-May, it was already getting uncomfortably hot in the afternoon. Roy and Rowdy were entered in the halter class for stallions and geldings, which was one of the first events in the morning. None of us wanted to wait all day for the riding competitions in the afternoon, so I signed up for the same class with Duke.

Among our competitors was Tornado's Sawdust, the beautifully metallic palomino stallion that I admired at the previous year's Horse Expo. The contestants entered the ring and walked around the arena a few times, closely watched by the judges, and then we lined up in the middle. Roy had Rowdy park out, while Duke and I just stood still in the lineup because Duke wasn't trained to park out. Although Roy's presentation of his horse was much better than mine, Duke had ideal conformation for a Fox Trotter. Most of the time, horses that are stallions have great conformation, as the majority of males are gelded, and generally only the best male horses are allowed to breed. After all, most people don't want to deal with the dangers of handling a stallion unless there is profit involved, and there isn't any money to be made in breeding low-quality horses.

In the halter class, Roy once again received a pink fifth-place ribbon, while Duke left the arena with the blue of first place pinned to his halter. The ebony former-stallion had already proven his merit by the dozens of superb foals he had produced, and the blood of World Grand Champion Fox Trotters flowed through his veins. To my surprise, he had edged out the only true competition in the show, the beautiful stallion Sawdust, who was the northern California halter champion.

Because both Roy and I placed, we qualified for the championship halter class, which was open to any horse—whether it was a mare, stallion, gelding, colt, or filly—that received fifth place or higher in any of the previous halter classes. The championship halter class was the same as the previous halter class, except the field of competitors was larger and consisted only of horses that were already proven winners.

When we all lined up in the center, however, Duke was distracted by the other horses in the class. While he was no longer physically capable of mating, he still had nearly a decade of learned courting behavior, and the close proximity of the mares captured his attention. When he was a stallion, almost all of his interaction with other horses was when he was breeding mares, and he was clearly interested in approaching and flirting with the nearby mares. Instead of standing still, he stepped from side to side, pivoted back and forth, and nearly broke out of line completely. The restlessness of my horse cost me, and we were demoted to second place, losing the blue ribbon to the seasoned show stallion Sawdust, who was used to the distractions of mares who were close at hand but off-limits in the show ring.

What was remarkable about the day was Roy's placement in the championship round. Despite the increased number of competitors, once again Roy proudly left with a fifth-place ribbon hung on Rowdy's halter.

The next month, June, was to be the grand finale of Roy's public horse showing career; he was coming with Mom and me as we returned to the Horse Expo as exhibitors for the last time. Mom was finally out of the horse business, and it was too much time, money, and effort to exhibit at the Horse Expo if we were only participating for fun. But it was worth going one last time, mostly due to Roy's unexpected role at the Expo.

Roy wasn't coming along as a mere spectator that year, but he also wasn't going to be a part of the breed showcase with Mom and me. Instead, Roy was one of the featured trainers, and he had a time slot for a round pen training exhibition every day. Several trainers were featured each year at the Horse Expo, including well-known names such as Clinton Anderson and John Lyons. Roy wasn't ever going to be a world-renowned horse trainer like them, but he had a training spot just as they did, albeit in a round pen instead of the main show arena.

John Segale was instrumental in getting Roy a training opportunity at the Expo. He lived in Elk Grove, which is the home to Project R.I.D.E. (Riding Instruction Designed for Education), a therapeutic riding center. It is a phenomenal facility, with a thirty-four-thousand-square-foot equestrian center that is fully enclosed and features both heating and air conditioning, as well as a fifty-two-acre ranch where the horses get to rest and relax when they aren't working. The motto of Project R.I.D.E. is "harnessing the magic to change lives," and they specialize in giving disabled students the opportunity to learn to ride. For many of the students, riding a horse is the only way they'll ever be able to feel what it is like to walk. For both students who are capable of walking and those who are unable, building a relationship with a horse and learning to direct it is an amazingly uplifting and empowering experience.

John had contacts at Project R.I.D.E., and he connected Roy with the people in charge of the organization. They were thrilled to have Roy as a partner for their booth at the Horse Expo, where they gave out pamphlets and information about their organization. Mom ordered a fresh batch of business cards for Roy to hand out, and we began to prepare for the Expo.

Rowdy had refused to eat and drink the year before, so it was unthinkable for us to bring him again, despite the fact that Roy had spent the most time working with him. Instead, Mom had Roy begin training with Duke, a calculated risk since Duke had been gelded only a few months before. He no longer had the rampant hormones of a stallion, but he still had the vestiges of behavior that he had learned throughout his lifetime as a breeding stud. Mom pinned her hopes on him being suitable for the Expo, because he would have to serve double duty that year, both as Roy's round pen horse and as Mom's riding mount for the Fox Trotter breed exhibition.

I was, of course, bringing Cassie again. We had come a long way in the past year. No longer would we be relegated to the end of the line, the tagalong baby team. Instead, we were going to lead the pack, not only setting the pace but also carrying the American flag.

I practiced flag tricks at home, whipping a piece of cloth on a stick around myself and my horse in a series of complex twists and flourishes. I wouldn't be performing any of them at the Expo, but they served to give me practice at controlling Cassie with one hand and the flag with the other, and they helped Cassie become completely comfortable with the flapping piece of cloth above her head.

Just like the prior year, we arrived at the fairground and put our horses in stalls in the Fox Trotter section. I hung the same handmade sign on Cassie's stall, and then Roy, Mom, and I went in search of the round pen where Roy would give his training demonstration.

We found the pen and immediately saw two huge problems: While the administrators had promised a sixty-foot diameter round pen, the area designated for Roy's training demonstration was actually a small square arena with eighty-foot sides. Both these factors can cause a great deal of difficulty when attempting round pen training, because a horse will often get "stuck" in the corners with its head facing out and its rump toward the trainer, looking for an escape, instead of making the turn and following the fence line. The greater distance to the center of the pen (fifty-five feet from the corner, nearly twice as far as in a standard round pen) makes it much more difficult for the trainer to firmly convey his commands to the horse. While the obstacle of having a square pen can be overcome and the horse taught to continue moving, Roy had a limited time for his demonstration, and the goal was to show more advanced elements of round pen training, not the relatively basic task of keeping the horse moving in a square pen.

Mom left Roy and me at the small arena while she went looking for an authority figure to tell about the problem. She came back with a man driving a golf cart loaded with wooden sawhorses. We placed the sawhorses in the corners, attempting to form a pseudo-fence line with the short barricades, but there weren't enough sawhorses to make more than a shabby fence with gaps plenty wide enough for a determined horse to push through. But it was all we had, so it would have to do.

Roy got Duke out of his stall and practiced in the makeshift round pen. Duke managed to navigate the corners fairly smoothly after receiving a little encouragement from Roy, but that was without the additional crowd, noises, smells, and distractions of the upcoming Expo.

Roy's first training demonstration was scheduled for eleven thirty Friday morning, a prime time because by then the Expo had been open long enough for a good crowd, but it was before the afternoon heat. The Fox Trotters were due in the breed showcase arena at the exact same time that day, so Duke's first performance in front of crowds would be with Roy, and Mom wouldn't ride until Saturday.

The makeshift round pen wasn't set aside for Roy's exclusive use. During the rest of the day, it was used for a handful of other scheduled training events or open for anyone's use as a warmup arena. Roy's demonstration on Friday was the first time the arena was scheduled for official use, so that morning it was free to be used by any equestrian who wanted it.

At a quarter past eleven, I swung into Cassie's saddle and lined up with the rest of the Fox Trotters, ready for our turn in the breed demonstrators' arena. I waved to Roy, who was leading Duke away toward his almost-round pen, lead rope in one hand, brand-new training flag—which hadn't been mauled and chewed by youngsters who got ahold of it when our backs were turned—in the other hand. With him was an entourage of some of his closest friends: Mom, Steve, and Al Roth, the former jockey.

"Good luck, Roy!" I called, and then was handed a flag of my own—not a small bit of black plastic on the end of a dressage whip, but an aluminum pole topped by a bronze eagle, the red, white, and blue of Old Glory streaming gently in the slight breeze. Cassie and I were dressed to match: I wore a spotless white shirt with a red bow tie at the collar, Cassie's bridle had red shining on the brow-band and caveson, and the Fox Trotter ribbons adorning her mane were red and blue.

When the clock struck eleven thirty, we moved to the side so the Shire horses before us could easily exit the arena. Then, as the announcer proclaimed our breed, Cassie and I entered the arena at a foxtrot, flag unfurling boldly behind us as the other horses and riders followed our pace and lead. I smiled broadly as we circled the arena and did a few patterns, before lining up and halting in the center like the year before. Since I was carrying the flag, I couldn't stand on my saddle and bow like I had previously—perhaps the true intention behind making me the official flag-bearer. But I didn't care; a thirteen-year-old girl and her four-year-old mare had led the pack.

At the same time as I was foxtrotting around the large arena, Roy was beginning his training demonstration in his improvised round pen. When he arrived at the arena, a group of horses was just exiting after warming up. They left behind evidence of their presence: several large piles of road apples. This wouldn't have been cause for concern, except for the fact that Duke was a recently gelded horse.

Manure is interesting to any horse; they like to smell it in order to find out information about other horses. For a stallion, however, smelling manure is a vital obsession. Each pile is a treasure trove of information about other horses in the area—either stallions, which are potential rivals, or mares, which are potential mates. By exhibiting what is called the Flehmen Response, a rather comical-looking gesture where they smell manure or urine, raise their head, and curl their upper lip back over their nostrils, scrunching their nose in a bizarre grin, stallions are even able to determine if a mare is in heat and therefore potentially sexually receptive.

Stallions will also use manure to mark their territory, making mounds of feces called stud piles, which they will add to daily. For domestic stallions, that behavior makes it easy to clean their stalls, as they will defecate in one large pile, rather than all over their pen like most geldings. Even though he was no longer a stallion, Duke still made a stud pile in his pen, still sniffed every pile of manure he encountered, and still frequently exhibited the Flehmen Response.

Duke also reacted to our mares whenever they came into heat at home; he nickered in the low, throaty grumble of a stallion when he caught their scent, arching his heavily muscled neck and prancing along the fence line to show off his prowess. He had not tried to breed a mare since he was gelded, but that was only because we had kept him separated from our mares. It wouldn't be until the year following the Expo that Duke would lose the last of his characteristic stallion behaviors.

When Roy entered the round pen and set Duke loose, the gleaming ebony horse immediately zeroed in on a pile of manure and took a long whiff, then raised his head high, upper lip curling back to expose his yellowed teeth, eyes rolling back in pleasure. Roy handed the halter and lead rope to Mom, who told him, "Remember your first lesson: Be more interesting than horse manure!" The comment made both of them laugh, taking the edge off Roy's nerves.

Roy turned and walked toward Duke, flicking the flag at him. Duke looked over his shoulder at the man approaching him, deciding whether or not he wanted to listen. Every line in Roy's body was determined; he wasn't going to accept any disobedience, especially not in front of an audience. Duke leapt forward, moving along the rail in a circle as he had been taught. He eyeballed another pile of manure in his path as he drew near it, but Roy wouldn't back down. Even though he averaged over forty feet from the horse, instead of under thirty feet like usual, Roy kept Duke moving and focused on him in the center of the square ring.

As Duke foxtrotted around the arena, he kept his head cocked toward Roy, watching his movements and waiting for a command. He ignored the wooden sawhorses in the corners, even though he could have squeezed between them in an effort to get out of work. His body bent toward the inside, following the curve of the round pen, and his inside ear was turned toward Roy; these were all signals Roy was looking for, body language that indicates that a horse is paying attention and attempting to do what is asked.

Roy took two steps back, lowering the flag, and Duke, sensing the relief of pressure, turned toward the center and Roy. But it wasn't a break like Duke had hoped; Roy stepped forward again, flag raised in his opposite hand, and Duke moved away, once again foxtrotting along the rail, but in the other direction. Mom narrated on a microphone, explaining to the small crowd what Roy was doing and how he was directing the horse as the training demonstration continued.

For Roy's friend Al, who had spent years racing horses at the track, the round pen training was astounding. He knew the challenges of working with stallions; unlike with horses ridden for pleasure, a much higher percentage of racehorses are kept as stallions because the breeding rights to a winning stallion are so lucrative; at the time, Northern Dancer held the world record for highest stud fee, at one million dollars per breeding in the 1980s. By comparison, the stud fee for a high-quality Fox Trotter is between five hundred and a thousand dollars. Consequently, racehorse jockeys have plenty of experience riding stallions, even ill-tempered and vicious stallions. In that industry, a winning record and the potential to make money on stud fees is often more important than a horse's dangerous temperament, especially since the owners themselves aren't the ones actually handling the horses.

Al watched Duke move freely around the pen, obeying Roy's commands willingly and immediately. Roy had no treats to bribe the horse, or ropes connected to Duke to tell him what to do; it was the partnership between the two that caused Duke to look to Roy for leadership, rather than looking to the outside of the pen for an escape from the work.

Finally Roy took a step back and didn't ask Duke to turn away when the horse turned to the center again. Duke didn't hesitate as he walked the entire forty feet to the center and stopped in front of Roy. Roy reached out his arms to welcome Duke, patting his neck as Duke lowered his head and licked his lips in contentment. Watching from his seat in the small bleachers, Al cried tears of joy at his friend's success.

After a moment, Roy turned away. Duke's head shot up, ears pricked forward as he watched to see if Roy was going to send him away and make him work again. When Roy took a step away, back turned to the horse, Duke mimed his action, following in Roy's footsteps. Even when they approached the fence—and the crowd on the other side—Duke didn't shy away. He wasn't accustomed to baby strollers, shopping bags, or large groups of people, but he was focused on following Roy. He knew if he got "unhooked" from Roy that he would have to start working again.

Roy turned sharply and headed directly toward Duke's rear end, but Duke wheeled, planting his front feet and swinging his back end around, so that his head stayed just behind Roy's hip the entire time. Roy changed tactics and walked toward Duke's shoulder. Duke moved out of his way, this time planting his back legs and swinging his front end away from Roy, maintaining the same distance from Roy at all times—not leaving Roy, but also keeping out of the invisible bubble that was Roy's space.

Then Roy raised the flag, and Duke was off again, moving around the pen at whatever speed Roy indicated: walk, foxtrot, or canter. After several more minutes of demonstrating different round pen techniques, Roy's time was up and he caught Duke and took him back to the stables.

This time, as Roy left the ring, he didn't question his performance. As Mom came to congratulate him, Roy didn't ask how well he had done; instead, he stated confidently, "I did good."

Mom gave him a hug. "Yes, you did."

By then, it was noon, and I had just finished putting Cassie back in her stall, so after Roy released Duke in his stall next to her, we went in search of a lunch of greasy fair food. Afterward, we found the booth for Project R.I.D.E. in the "Mane Marketplace," a huge building filled with exhibitors' booths. The setup for Project R.I.D.E. ended up being just around the corner from the Pacific Coast Fox Trotter Association's booth, which members were supposed to volunteer to man throughout the three-day weekend. As one of the youth riders, I was thankfully exempted from that onerous task.

Roy, on the other hand, was delighted to stay at Project R.I.D.E.'s booth, underneath a large banner that bore his name and proclaimed him as the featured trainer for the organization. He enjoyed the rest of the day sipping a blue pop in the air-conditioned building, greeting all the fairgoers passing by and encouraging them to donate time, money, and resources to Project R.I.D.E. for the benefit of the disabled children they served.

I spent the weekend of the Horse Expo much the same as I had the year prior: wandering through the conglomerate of vendors in the various barns and warehouses, watching a few harness races at the track, cooling off next door at Waterworld, and admiring the various horse breeds featured at the Expo. I attended a couple of training demonstrations but didn't stay long, as the afternoon heat was quick to drive me back into the havens of the air-conditioned buildings.

On Saturday, Roy's demonstration was at eleven in the morning, while the Fox Trotters didn't ride until five forty-five that evening, so Mom and Roy were both able to use Duke for their events. Roy's morning demonstration went just as well as the previous day, and after Duke was back in his stall, we went in search of lunch. As Roy and Mom walked down the wide dirt thoroughfare near the stables, one of the world-renowned trainers rode his horse up behind them, heading toward the main arena. Ironically, one of his demonstrations that year was themed around love, language, and leadership, but he rode through the Expo like it was his own private trail, heedless of the people around him except to bask in their admiring looks.

The trainer plowed through the crowd, apparently expecting everyone to move out of his way, including the slowly shuffling older gentleman in his path. Roy was oblivious to the danger bearing down on him from behind. Although equestrians technically have the right-of-way and pedestrians are supposed to yield to them, common courtesy and a regard for the safety of others is usually present in riders. The trainer could have easily ridden his horse at the edge of the crowd and thus avoided most of the pedestrians traversing the thoroughfare, but instead it seemed he reveled in attracting as much attention as possible.

Mom turned and saw the approaching horse and rider when they were just a few strides away, Roy directly in their path. She grabbed Roy's arm and hustled him out of the way in the nick of time, the trainer continuing on his way as if nothing had happened, either senselessly oblivious or heedlessly indifferent to the fact that he had nearly run over Roy.

Mom was furious, intent on following the trainer and giving him a verbal lashing for how close he came to hitting Roy with his horse, but Roy stopped her.

"I'm okay, it's not worth getting upset over," he told Mom. "You getting angry about it hurts you more than it hurts him."

"You're right, Roy, thank you," Mom replied. "Sometimes I let my temper get a little out of control. Thank you for helping me calm down."

As the long day drew to a close, Mom and I prepared Duke and Cassie for our evening demonstration with the Fox Trotters. Since Duke still expressed some stallion-like behaviors, I kept Cassie away from him as we warmed up in open space behind the stables; after all, I had no desire to risk my mare being mounted while I was riding her. Though Cassie was only four, we had made great strides in our training together over the last year. She no longer needed a buddy to follow for emotional support, and we had no problems striking out on our own.

As I rode around, I was approached by a man and his young son, who looked to be about six. "Can my boy get a picture on your horse?"

I was taken aback by the request, but I had seen John Segale lead a kid around on Domo earlier. "Sure, I guess," I replied and swung down from the saddle.

The man lifted the boy onto Cassie's saddle. I smiled for the picture, then led Cassie around in a big circle to give the child a chance to experience what it felt like to ride a moving horse. When I was done, the man lifted his son down, thanked me, and walked away.

As I remounted my horse, Mom came riding over. "You shouldn't have done that," she scolded.

"I saw John do it earlier," I said, surprised to be getting in trouble.

"Well that's his choice," Mom replied. "But if that kid had fallen off and gotten hurt, his dad could have sued us. That didn't happen, but don't do that again."

"Okay," I said, my face burning red. "Sorry."

"It's all right; you didn't know you shouldn't do that."

It was almost time for our demonstration, so we lined up near the arena gate. I took my place at the head of the line and was handed my flag; Mom placed Duke near the rear of the line, behind a gelding instead of a mare. The gates swung open, the previous riders exited the arena, and we entered at a foxtrot, parading around the arena then lining up in the center as usual.

After the Fox Trotter breed demonstration was finished and we were untacking our horses, I was approached by a middle-aged woman.

"Your horse is so beautiful," she chirped.

"Thank you."

"How old is she?"

"She's four."

"Wow, that's so young to be at the Expo! She's doing very well. Who trained her?"

"Well, I started her right after I turned twelve, and then Bryan Neubert put sixty days of training on her. But other than that, I'm the only one who rides her. We rode at the Expo last year too."

"That's amazing! I've been looking for a really gentle horse to ride. She sounds wonderful. How much will you take for her?"

"Cassie is not for sale," I replied firmly.

"What about if I offer you ten thousand dollars?"

"She's still not for sale."

"You're pretty young to be making a decision like that. Why don't you ask your mom and think about it overnight. I'll be here tomorrow."

"Cassie is my horse, and I'm not selling her," I said, but the lady didn't seem to hear me as she smiled and walked away.

I told Mom about the offer when we were driving home.

"I've seen that woman riding before," Mom said. "She's a very beginner rider. She doesn't realize that a large part of the way Cassie behaves is because you ride her so well. She'd get into trouble quick if she rode Cassie. Besides, you'd regret it for the rest of your life if you sold Cassie."

"I know," I said. "I told her Cassie isn't for sale."

"Yes, but it sounds like you'll hear from her again. It's a bit offensive that she was so dismissive of you and wants to go behind your back to talk to me. Cassie is your horse, and you can do what you want with her. I'm proud that you stood up to that woman."

The rest of the weekend ran smoothly, with Roy and Duke performing harmoniously in the makeshift round pen, and the Fox Trotter breed demonstrations going on without a hitch. Cassie and I continued to be the flag-bearers for the group, leading the head-bobbing, mane-shaking, ribbon-bedecked group. True to her word, the woman who wanted to buy Cassie showed up again, strongly hinting that she was willing to pay twice as much for my mare. I flatly refused, and it finally sunk in that I was serious. She left, a look of frustration and dejection on her face.

At last, the final day of the HorseExpo wound to a close, and we loaded the horses in the trailer and brought them home from CalExpo for the last time, the grande finale of show careers for all three of us. It was time to move on to a new stage of equestrian life, and Roy was about to get the present of a lifetime.

Chapter 12
A Cowboy's Saddle

LATER THAT SUMMER, Mom purchased Steve's silver Honda Civic to be Brian's high school car. Mom felt that Steve had asked for too low a price, so she decided to make up for the cost by buying Roy a saddle. More than just a present of leather and wood, it was a gift of love and a promise for the future.

When John Segale heard that Roy was getting a saddle, he had Mom send it to him before she gave it to Roy. John then paid to have the saddle customized to be more like a true cowboy's saddle. John had the stirrups turned so that they wouldn't hurt Roy's knees as they were being broken in, and he had both the lower part of the stirrups and the horn wrapped in leather.

The end result was a simple but stylish western saddle. Made of beautiful brown leather, it had basket-weave tooling on nearly every surface: the pommel crowned by the horn, the cheyenne roll on the back edge of the seat, the rounded skirt, the fenders of each stirrup, and even the billet straps for a rear cinch, which Roy never used because he wasn't going to be doing any abrupt work like roping or cutting cattle from a herd. The seat of the saddle was smooth, padded black leather, while the horn was wrapped with soft, cream-colored suede, like ropers used to protect their saddle horns when they dallied their ropes.

The only difference between Roy's saddle and a standard western saddle was the skirt, which was small and rounded to accommodate the short backs of gaited horses, rather than the typical square-cut Quarter horse saddles, which would have interfered with the hip and leg movement of the long-striding Fox Trotters. This standard alteration for smooth-gaited horses also shaved several pounds off Roy's saddle, making it easier to swing onto a horse's back.

The new saddle was elegant, but it was a tool to be used, not something to just look at. Mom wasn't just giving Roy a saddle, she was giving him a promise that she was finally going to teach him to ride a horse. Although she was still worried about Roy having a seizure if he fell off, she realized that Roy understood the risk and it was his choice to assume it.

Roy didn't get to use his saddle for a while, as Mom gave it to him around Christmas, and the weather was too cold and wet for ideal riding conditions. The months of January and February are usually filled with back-to-back rainstorms, broken by short days of sunlight that are barely enough to dry the sodden, muddy ground before more gray clouds roll in again. Consequently, Roy's saddle sat unused in our tack room until spring, protected from dust and cat scratches by a black nylon cover.

A few months after Roy received his saddle, he and Mom went to a colt-starting clinic that Bryan Neubert was teaching about one and a half hours from Winters, relatively close compared to most of his other clinic locations around the country. Roy hadn't seen Neubert since they first met in Reno, but the two men occasionally spoke on the phone and Neubert was always encouraging Roy in his round pen endeavors.

Mom was going to the clinic as a spectator, rather than bringing a horse along to train, so she picked up Roy in the morning, driving Steve's old Civic. Squeezed into the trunk was Roy's new saddle, which Roy wanted to show to Neubert and get his opinion about. Along the way, they stopped at Lester Farms Bakery and bought sausage-and-cheese croissants for breakfast.

When they finally reached the clinic, it had already begun. Mom paid her admission, but when she tried to pay for Roy, she was informed that Neubert had arranged for Roy to watch for free. They headed over to the round pen, where spectators already filled the bleachers.

At this particular clinic, the round pen walls were not made of pipe panels, which would allow onlookers to look through the fence, but instead consisted of six-foot-high solid wood fences. The bleachers for the spectators to sit in were raised above the fence, so onlookers were looking down into the round pen. Mom and Roy made their way to the top of the stairs at the back of the stands and then wound through the bleachers, which were mostly filled, looking for a good seat.

Neubert looked up and saw them enter. He paused in his training demonstration.

"Hi, Roy," he said, his voice amplified by the headset microphone he wore. "That man up there is my friend, Roy," he told the crowd. "He is someone that you should take the time to meet." The crowd turned to look at Roy and Mom.

"Cheryl, how's that black stud of yours doing?" Neubert asked Mom.

"He's doing real well," Mom called back.

Neubert had trained Duke back in 1998, when Mom purchased the four-year-old stallion. At the time of the clinic, Duke had already been gelded, and he was turning into a fun, reliable trail horse for Mom.

"Good," Neubert replied. "I love that horse."

Neubert resumed working with the horse he had in the round pen with him, finishing the clinic without further comment to Mom or Roy. Afterward, he went out to the parking lot with them to see Roy's new saddle.

"That's a real fine saddle, Roy," Neubert said, as Roy beamed. "I'm sure you'll have fun learning how to ride, and you'll look great with this saddle."

As Mom and Roy finally got into the car to leave, Mom noticed that Roy was chewing on something.

"What are you eating, Roy?" she asked.

"The sausage croissant," he replied. "I didn't want to finish it earlier, but I'm hungry now."

Mom was horrified. The croissant, filled with easily-spoiled cheese and meat, had been sitting in the hot car all afternoon, and Mom was certain that it was festering with bacteria.

"You'd better not get sick, Roy," she said jokingly. "I don't want to have to take you to the hospital."

"Don't worry, I have a cast-iron stomach," he replied.

Fortunately, Roy didn't get food poisoning, and he stayed healthy enough to finally begin his highly anticipated riding lessons later that week.

At first, Mom tried having Roy ride Rowdy. Mom had Roy climb onto a low haystack, and then she held Rowdy close to it while he clambered into the saddle. Then she led Roy and Rowdy to the round pen, which was a small, safe area for any beginner learning to ride, since the horse would never be far from the trainer on the ground.

With Rowdy still on a lead rope, Mom refreshed Roy on the basics of controlling a horse from its back: pull on the left rein to turn left, the right rein to turn right, and both reins to stop. With Rowdy, there was an additional consideration: "*Never* kick this horse, Roy," Mom told him. "You know how sensitive he is to you asking him to speed up when you are doing round pen training? He is exactly the same way when you are riding him. If you want to speed up, all you have to do is barely squeeze him with your legs. Sometimes, he will even go faster if you just squeeze your butt muscles. So if you kick him, you'll end up in the next county."

Roy laughed, but made an effort to not touch the horse with his legs at all when he was riding. Mom had set up cones in the round pen for Roy to practice steering around and through, and she initially kept Rowdy on a lead line while Roy practiced. Mom wasn't controlling Rowdy's direction with the lead rope—in fact, sometimes Roy had to assert his authority when Rowdy wanted to follow directly after Mom but Roy wanted him to weave through the cones first—but the lead rope allowed Mom to make sure Rowdy didn't speed up when Roy wasn't prepared for it. After a while, Roy gained enough confidence in his ability to control the horse that he asked Mom to remove the lead rope.

Once Rowdy was set loose in the round pen, it quickly became apparent that he was not an appropriate horse for Roy to learn to ride. Since Rowdy knew he was under the sole control of the rider, and not constrained by a lead rope, he began obeying the minuscule, unintentional commands that Roy was giving for him to speed up. He didn't take off at a gallop, or even a foxtrot, but he did continually speed up into a gaited walk, and Roy would then have to pull back on the reins and slow him down. The fairly quick fluctuations in speed were enough to make it difficult for Roy to stay balanced atop the tall horse, and Roy worried that he would fall off.

The fear of falling caused Roy's muscles to tense instinctively in the face of danger. That tightness transmitted through the saddle to the sensitive skin of the horse, who took it as a cue to speed up, making it even more difficult for Roy to keep Rowdy at a walk.

They decided to stop for the day, but were immediately faced with a new problem: how to get Roy safely off the tall horse. It was too risky to have Roy climb off on the haystack, since if Rowdy took a single step away from the hay while Roy was dismounting, he would fall directly underneath the horse. Fortunately, at that moment Jesús, Mom's trusted ranch hand, who had been working at Red Tail Farm almost since the beginning, arrived at the ranch and was able to help Roy swing out of the saddle and slide slowly down to the ground in a controlled manner.

After Mom took Roy home that afternoon, she was left to ponder her dilemma of which horse to use to teach Roy how to ride. She had promised Roy that he could ride, but Rowdy, while a phenomenal horse for Roy to learn to round pen train, was clearly an inappropriate choice. Mom considered all the horses remaining in the herd: Duke was prone to spinning abruptly when startled by something, like a rabbit jumping out of the bushes, and was quite successful at unseating even Mom with his athleticism; Cassie was my horse, and I had trained her to be very sensitive to leg commands, like Rowdy; Damien was aging and too small for Roy to ride; and Rokko was too young and green.

The only horse left was Rain Dance, Mom's prodigal mare that she sold to the Segales in lieu of selling my favorite mare, DeeDee. A couple of years after they bought Rain Dance, she got into a kick fight with another of their mares. Neither was seriously injured, but the Segales decided they didn't want to deal with mares that wanted to kick each other, and one of them had to go. John called Mom and brought Rain Dance back to Red Tail Farm, taking a young gelding in trade.

Mom hadn't cried when she sold Rain Dance, but she cried tears of joy when her mare was returned. She spent the whole afternoon bathing and brushing the gray mare, scrubbing her dappled coat and bleaching her yellowed tail back to a pure, gleaming white.

Mom decided that Rain Dance would be a good horse for Roy to learn to ride since the mare was small, so it would be easier to heave Roy into the saddle, but she was still big enough to easily carry him. She was also as sweet and gentle as she looked, although she was a bit on the lazy side, which made her less fun for an experienced rider but safer for a beginner.

To make it even easier to get Roy, who, besides being short, isn't the most graceful person around, into the saddle, one of Roy's friends built a special mounting block for him. Most mounting blocks are portable and plastic, with two steps and a top that is only a couple square feet for the rider to stand on while mounting. Roy's mounting block needed to be big enough that he would have a sturdy platform to both mount and dismount from the horse, so he wouldn't have to slide all the way to the ground when getting off. The mounting block that was built was made of solid wood, with three steps and a top platform that was three by four feet. It required at least two people or the tractor to move it, but portability wasn't a necessity for Roy. The mounting block was placed near the gate to the arena, a perfect location for Roy to swing into the saddle since it was just a few steps away from the safety of the sandy enclosure.

Roy only got the opportunity to ride Rain Dance a few times. Despite the mare's gentle nature, she had a tolerance level for how long she let Roy ride each day. The most difficult task for any beginning rider to master isn't how to control the horse, it's how to stay balanced atop a moving, swaying animal that rocks its rider from side to side with every step. Rain Dance wasn't appreciative of having a full-grown man off-balance atop her, and after a half hour of Roy riding, she would start to get cranky, pinning her ears and swishing her tail in annoyance. Neither Roy nor Mom wanted to test Rain Dance's reactions if Roy continued to ride longer, so the riding lessons gradually came to a halt, and Roy's saddle once again sat unused in the tack room, waiting for the right time and the right horse.

In the meantime, Roy and Steve decided to take a road trip to Colorado in order to visit Grandpa Bill and Grandma Lulu, who invited them to visit every time they saw the Irwin brothers during their trips to California.

Once the brothers arrived at the Lundberg home in Cedaredge, Roy learned, to his dismay, that Mom hadn't fallen too far from the family tree. Throughout their friendship, Mom had always pushed Roy to become more independent and capable of doing things for himself. Despite the fact that Roy was already in his early sixties when they met, Mom often treated him like one of her own children. Mom had always made a very conscious choice to raise Brian and me to be as independent and resourceful as possible. This child-rearing strategy didn't mean abandoning us to our own devices, but rather pushing us outside our comfort zone when we wanted something—"You can have the toy, Lauren, but you need to ask the lady behind the counter for it. Here is some money. You can pay for it yourself."

It didn't take long for Mom to decide to "raise" Roy as well, and Roy was eager to have a new mother-figure in his life; after all, he had lived with Glenys until her death when Roy was fifty-three years old. It was with some consternation that Roy learned Mom wasn't going to treat him the way Glenys did. When Roy asked for help putting a halter on Rowdy, Mom wouldn't take over and do it for him. Instead, she would demonstrate how to put it on the horse properly, then take it off again and have Roy do it himself. "I have faith in you, Roy. You can do it," she encouraged him.

Mom would then pretend to not watch him and allow him to attempt to figure it out and struggle a bit before intervening again. Sometimes Roy would cry, but Mom would hug him and help him start again, until he finally succeeded in tying the rope halter correctly. Mom reassured Roy many times that anything worth taking pride in accomplishing was hard to do and required perseverance; it was normal to feel frustrated while learning something difficult.

Roy knew that Mom's decision to teach him to be more independent helped him overcome the biggest challenge he faced his entire life. He admitted, "People always did things for me because they thought I couldn't. That's where I got screwed up, because if they didn't do anything, I would've learned." But despite knowing this, it was still challenging for him to put it into action and step out of his comfort zone.

Pushing people out of their comfort zone was a family trait, as Roy soon learned. The first evening of his and Steve's trip to Colorado, Roy wanted to take a shower, and he asked Grandma Lulu for a bath towel.

"They're in the closet in the bathroom, Roy," Grandma said. "Use any towel you want."

Roy went to the bathroom, but he didn't see any closet or towels. The closet door was directly adjacent to the entrance to the bathroom, and when the bathroom door was open, it hid the closet from sight.

Roy left the bathroom and returned to where Grandma was folding laundry.

"I can't find the towels," he said. "Can you just get one for me, please?"

Grandma responded exactly the same way her daughter would have: kindly but firm, with no room for argument. "You can do it, Roy. Go in the bathroom and close the door. Then you'll see the closet door and you can get a towel out."

Roy couldn't believe Grandma would be a stern taskmaster of a hostess, but he returned to the bathroom and finally found the towels.

For the rest of the trip, Grandma made the Irwins very welcome, cooking breakfast and dinner for them every day and giving them ideas of fun things to do locally during their visit. But Roy knew he wouldn't be able to get away with asking her to do something that he could do himself. After a week in Colorado, the brothers drove back to California. By then, the summer was drawing to a close, ushering in a new school year with a new set of challenges. Roy's classroom speaking career was about to expand to the nearby towns, and I was leaving behind the Winters school system forever.

Chapter 13
The Right Words

AS I WAS beginning my first year of high school, Roy was starting his second year as a classroom speaker. Since I was no longer attending Winters Middle School, it wasn't feasible for me to skip one class and attend Roy's talks, especially since his territory had expanded as he had hoped. That year, he was scheduled to speak in classrooms at many different schools located in the towns near Winters, including Woodland, Davis, and Dixon, as well as at the Winters Middle School. For Roy's talk in Dixon, Roy and Mom didn't bring Roy's training video for the visual demonstration. Instead, they brought Rowdy for a live training exhibition.

The week before the Dixon demonstration, Mom used the horse trailer to haul several semi-portable pipe-panel fence sections to make a small round pen on the school grounds. It was just large enough for Rowdy to foxtrot in a circle, but a little too small for the big horse to easily canter. The smaller pen also presented a challenge to Roy in his role as a trainer—due to the tight quarters, every command Roy gave to speed up would be more intense, making Rowdy more difficult to slow down and execute calm, gentle turns. But by then, the horse and man were so in sync with one another that the round pen presentation went without a hitch. Roy used his soft, subtle commands to direct Rowdy to do his bidding in a flawless performance.

The real challenge came in the classroom. Two of the boys sauntered inside to slouch in their desks at the back of the room, sneers of scorn and derision on their faces. They reluctantly stopped talking when their teacher called the class to order, but it was clear from every nuance of their body language that they were neither impressed by the horse running around in a circle, nor interested in hearing what the stuttering old man in front of them had to say.

Mom saw the reactions of the boys, and she braced herself for trouble; they were the same type of boys who had ridiculed and teased Roy so much when he was younger, and she expected them to disrupt Roy and make fun of him during his talk.

The boys smirked and muttered to one another as Roy began to speak, only quieting down when they caught the withering glare of their teacher.

"You might notice that I talk a little different," Roy began. The boys rolled their eyes—of course they had noticed. "When I was your age, I was made fun of and institutionalized because I was different. And it was hard. It hurt, and I was very angry."

Roy paused, and then he said something he hadn't said in any other classroom speech. Despite the fact that his dad could be harsh, and his parents had sent him to the institution, Roy always said that he felt loved by his parents, especially his overprotective and doting mother.

"How many of you know what it's like to not be loved by your mama and daddy?" Roy asked.

They were words that cut to the soul. Both boys dropped their gazes to their desks, not wanting anyone to see the pain that suddenly filled their eyes. The answer to the question was plain on their faces: I know.

"I know what that's like," Roy continued. "I know what it's like for your daddy to think you're a disappointment and to wish he had a different son. And it hurts. It hurts a lot.

"I want you to know that Jesus loves you, and I love you," Roy said firmly, and two pairs of eyes lifted to gaze hopefully at his face. "No matter what, even if you feel all alone in the world, God loves you, and he will be there for you. I know. Even when I was boozing and fighting, Jesus still loved me.

"People can be mean to you, but don't let them tell you what you can do. I never thought I could work with the horses or do round pen training. But if you put your mind to something, you can do it. Don't let people put you down or make you feel like you're worthless."

The two boys sat enraptured for the rest of Roy's talk, their entire attention focused on him. When Roy finished, the teacher asked for volunteers to serve cookies to the class. Immediately they both jumped up and came forward, grabbing the packages of cookies and taking them to Roy to serve him first. When the recess bell rang and the class filed out to the playground, Roy stood next to the doorway and offered to shake hands or give hugs to anyone that wanted them. The two boys gave Roy a quick but tight hug before heading outside.

A few weeks later, Roy spoke at Holmes Junior High in Davis. As the students sat in the darkened classroom and watched the video, occasional whispers from another pair of trouble-maker boys were audible. Despite a warning from the teacher, the boys continued to mutter and laugh under their breath.

When the video ended and the lights came back on, Roy stood up to speak. "I come to classrooms to talk because I hope that what I have to say will help you. School is hard, and it can be tough to keep trying. I want to encourage all of you to continue your studies and do the best that you can. But not everyone will hear what I have to say, and that's their loss. But if just one person listens and learns something, then I consider it worthwhile and a success."

Roy paused and looked directly at the two noisy boys. They quieted as he made eye contact with both of them. "I'm not getting paid to be here. So if you don't want to listen, there's the door." He pointed at the exit. "But either way, I want it quiet so everyone can listen without interruption."

The boys flushed with embarrassment; clearly they hadn't been expecting Roy to call them to task. They were the first to break eye contact with Roy, staring down at their desktops in submission. For the remainder of Roy's talk, they sat silently in their seats, listening to Roy rather than ridiculing him.

Roy was amazed by their acquiescence; the confidence at giving commands in the round pen was starting to show itself in other ways, granting him the power to act with authority when necessary. When he had encountered disruptive students the year before, he had gotten flustered, lost his train of thought, and avoided confronting the students, instead allowing their teacher to restore order and silence. Those days were behind him. The respect that he had received in the classroom gave Roy an exhilarating feeling of accomplishment that he would never forget.

Chapter 14
High School Hijinks

I WAS ACTIVELY involved in sports throughout my high school career, playing basketball all four years and softball when I was a freshman and sophomore. Mom often picked Roy up and brought him to games, both home and away, and he was an avid supporter from the sidelines. At softball games at VCS, there was only one small set of uncomfortable metal bleachers, so many of the parents of the players brought folding camping chairs to watch the game. During the spring softball season, Mom kept two chairs in the trunk of her car at all times, one for her and one for Roy.

Strong, gusty north winds that last for a few days are common in the Winters and Vacaville area. They fill the air with dirt, creating towering clouds of dust, and frequently knock down trees bordering the road leading to Red Tail Farm. Mom and Roy came to a softball game during one such windstorm, which had turned the day from cool and pleasant to bitingly cold and miserable.

During warmups, I saw Mom and Roy arrive, struggling to set up their folding chairs without them blowing away in the gusts. Fortunately, the wind was blowing from behind them, so they at least had the minuscule protection of the cloth chairs against their backs, and they didn't have to worry about grit flying into their eyes. They huddled deep in their chairs as the game began.

The players were suffering in the wind as well. We didn't have a dugout to provide us with shelter, just a bench behind the chain-link fence bordering the third base line. All of us wore long-sleeved shirts under our uniforms and had our team windbreakers zipped tight when we were waiting to play. Since we wore shorts instead of pants, we pulled the protective pads on our knees up high to give us some heat retention, instead of folding them over to keep them out of the way like we usually did when we weren't batting and running bases.

After the first inning, Mom came over to where I was watching the game and waiting for my turn at-bat. She always dressed in layers to keep warm, and Roy was wearing one of his Red Tail Farm sweatshirts, but with the howling wind, it wasn't enough.

"Lauren, do you have a sweatshirt or something in your bag? Roy and I are freezing."

"Yes, my letterman's jacket is in my bag. You can get it out." I turned back to watch the game, since the coach was giving me a dirty look for not paying attention, and let Mom get the jacket herself.

When I ran out on the field at the top of the next inning, I glanced over to where Mom and Roy were sitting. Apparently my letterman jacket hadn't been enough to keep them both warm, and Mom had plundered all my school clothes from my bag. Their chairs were shoved close together so they could share my jacket and t-shirt as blankets, but the icing on the cake was my jeans, the legs of which were draped across their shoulders like a bizarre scarf. They smiled and waved when I saw them; although they were pleased with their ingenuity, I was torn between amusement at their desperation and mortification at their strange attire.

Even scrounging all my clothes wasn't enough to keep them warm, however, and after another inning they retreated to the car, where they watched the remainder of the game. Afterward, a warm wool blanket was added to the trunk for future games.

Besides coming to my games, Roy spent a lot of time at Red Tail Farm. Every week, he and Steve came over for a Bible study with Mom and a couple of their friends. One morning, Mom told a story from the years she and Dad had lived in San Francisco.

"There was a newspaper column one day about a woman in Chinatown," Mom said. "She bought a live chicken, and she was going to take it home and cook it. But when she was getting on the bus, the bus driver said, 'No live animals.' So she smiled, wrung the chicken's neck, and got on the bus."

Roy and Steve, who was a bus driver in Sacramento at the time, laughed uproariously as they imagined the look on the poor bus driver's face.

"So, Steve, what would you do if someone tried to get on your bus with a live chicken?" Mom asked.

"I'd probably just let them on." Steve laughed.

The next week, while Steve was working, Roy, Mom, and I hatched a plan. I caught three of our chickens and put them in a dog carrier, which we loaded up in the Suburban and drove to Sacramento. We parked along Steve's bus route and sat at one of the bus stops, the crate of chickens at our feet. After a couple of phone calls to a very confused Steve to find out his exact location, we found out Steve was driving in the opposite direction of what we had thought. So we crossed the street and waited, waving on a few buses that tried to pick us up before we finally spotted Steve heading our way.

I quickly got the hens out of the crate and passed them to Roy and Mom, making sure their wings were clamped tightly to their bodies so they couldn't escape. We sat on the bench, squawking chickens in hand and wide smirks plastered across our faces as Steve pulled the bus to a stop in front of us.

"What are you doing?" Steve laughed. He couldn't believe his eyes. "Did you really bring chickens to Sacramento?"

"Yep." We laughed.

"I can't believe it! I was wondering why Roy was calling and asking me where I was. I thought maybe something had happened to him," Steve said, still laughing.

We put the chickens back in the dog carrier and gave Steve a hug goodbye, letting him get back to his route, and then laughed during our entire drive back home in remembrance of the look of surprise on his face. Once back at Red Tail Farm, we released the still-alive but probably very confused chickens back at the barn.

Later that year, our herd of horses increased. When Mom was selling all the horses, she had given three fillies to a contractor in exchange for a hay barn. Construction began immediately, but once the concrete foundation and steel frame of the hay barn were completed, the contractor stopped coming to Red Tail Farm and working on the building. When Mom called to see when he was planning on resuming his work, he always responded with the same excuse: "I'm really busy with other projects right now. I'll come out next month and finish it."

The hay barn soon became a major thorn in Mom's side. While the house and horse barn were painted in shades of grays and blues, the unfinished structure was an eye-smarting shade of reddish-orange, drawing everyone's gaze and making it the first thing that any visitor noticed.

Roy was especially fond of giving Mom a hard time about the incomplete structure. "So, when is the barn going to be finished?" he asked every time he visited the ranch and spotted the eyesore.

Finally Mom had enough of Roy's teasing. The next time she picked him up to run errands, he asked with a feigned innocence, "How's the barn coming along?"

Mom pulled the car to a stop on the side of the road, a few blocks from Roy's house. "Okay, Roy, you can get out here and walk home. I'll go shopping by myself."

Roy's only reaction was to laugh uproariously, pleased at eliciting a response from his teasing.

After over two years of waiting for the hay barn to be completed, Mom heard from a mutual friend that the contractor had sold one of the horses that he'd taken in trade. Mom hadn't signed the horses' registration papers to make the man their official owner, but if he managed to sell the other two without papers, there would be little that she could do to get them back. She immediately decided to repossess the other two horses and call off the deal.

When the two mares returned to Red Tail Farm, they were both old enough to be ridden, but neither had been trained to ride. Mom sold one of them to a trainer that was a friend of hers. Since I was too busy with school to train the other, she decided to send the second mare, Duchess of the Stars, to a professional trainer over the winter. Rokko, Cassie's younger brother, was three years old and ready to be started under saddle, so Mom sent him along as well. Bryan Neubert was too busy to train the two horses, so his son, Jimmy, rode them instead.

Mom had decided to keep Rokko instead of selling him, despite the fact that he didn't have much of a functional role on the ranch. I wasn't interested in him, since I had Cassie, and Mom preferred riding shorter horses. But besides Rowdy, Rokko was the only horse we had that was big enough to carry Dad on the rare occasions that Dad decided to ride, and Rowdy was aging. Rokko, on the other hand, was just beginning the prime of his life—a life full of purpose, as we would one day discover.

Chapter 15
Saying Goodbye

ALTHOUGH ROWDY WAS still a great horse for Mom to ride, both on the trail and in parades, Mom was worried because the big chestnut gelding's health wouldn't last forever. Mom didn't want to keep and feed a horse that was too old to be ridden, so she decided to sell Rowdy when he turned twenty, an age when he still had several more good years of gentle riding ahead of him.

Roy was devastated when he heard the news that Rowdy was going to be sold. The horse had been his constant companion as he struggled to master the art of round pen training, and Roy was one of the few people in the world that Rowdy trusted implicitly. But Rowdy had imparted all the lessons that he could to Roy, and in return Rowdy had learned that humans could be a source of kindness and gentleness instead of pain and fear. The journey they had taken together was complete, and it was time for them to begin their own voyages apart from one another.

On May 7, 2007, Rowdy left Red Tail Farm forever, to live a life of semi-retirement in the Oakland Hills. His new owners were looking for a horse to go on easy trail rides on weekends, and they had already nurtured a few retired horses into their thirties, a ripe old age for an equine. As Roy said a tearful goodbye to Rowdy, his new owners promised to send Roy pictures and updates, and they kept their word, sending Roy a Christmas card with pictures of his faithful horse every year.

Around the same time Mom sold Rowdy, we lent Damien to Project R.I.D.E. to be a therapeutic riding horse. It was the perfect occupation for the aging gelding: students brushed and pampered him, and only children who were small enough for him to easily carry were allowed to ride him. On weekends, he was turned out to pasture to frolic and graze. The students were especially enthralled by his nearly blind eye; like them, he had a disability, but it didn't stop him from being able to perform like all of the other horses.

Damien was a star at Project R.I.D.E., but he was only there on lease. When Grandma had given him to me, she made Mom promise that she would never sell or give away Damien. Because of that promise, Mom's name was still on his ownership papers, and after he was at Project R.I.D.E. for six months she realized that if any child got hurt while riding Damien, she could be held liable and get sued since she still owned him. So Damien came back to live at Red Tail Farm.

Not long afterward, Mom's side of the family came to visit for Christmas, including my cousin Jenna, who had learned to ride on Damien. Despite the cold weather, the skies were clear, so Jenna and I bundled up in several layers and went for a ride around the property every day. Damien enjoyed the slow, easy outings, carrying a young rider, but on our third ride, tragedy struck.

A patch of mud was hidden by a dense section of weeds, and Damien walked obliviously into the danger. The slick footing caught him off guard and he slipped, stumbling forward. Jenna was thrown off balance and started to fall from the saddle, but with a valiant effort Damien lunged forward so that she was once again centered on his back, keeping her from falling to the ground.

The strain was too much on Damien's aging tendons and ligaments, and when he had recovered his balance, he walked out of the muddy patch with a significant limp. I immediately jumped off my horse and helped Jenna to dismount.

"Are you okay?" I asked Jenna.

She was visibly shaken by the fright from almost falling, but she responded, "I'm fine."

Damien, on the other hand, was clearly in pain. We walked him slowly back to the barn, where we untacked him, gave him painkillers, and wrapped his legs with polo wraps to give his ligaments support.

For the next several months, Damien was given time off to recover. His initial injury healed, but as time passed, his overall condition worsened. Age was taking its toll on his body, and after a while, it was a struggle for him to stand up again whenever he lay down.

Horses don't fear death the way humans do; they have no understanding of the concept. What they do fear is pain, and the hardest situation is when a horse is suffering and will not recover. In that case, it is unfair to the animal to keep it alive just because we have a hard time saying goodbye to it. The best thing an owner can do for their faithful mount is to ensure that the ending is as painless as possible, and not keep the horse alive past the point where it enjoys living.

This knowledge doesn't make it any easier when the time to make that decision finally arrives, and it was with many tears that I trailered Damien to the vet for the last time. I unloaded him into a stall with fresh shavings, a clean bucket of water, and a flake of hay, and then I said goodbye to my noble little horse for the last time.

Chapter 16
Opening Eyes

ONE OF ROY'S lifelong challenges has been keeping his hoard of treasures—which Steve has dubbed the "Irwin Relics"—out of the way and somewhat organized. Roy is notorious for keeping every scrap of paper as a memento: postcards, magazines, restaurant menus, event programs, books, photographs and more are displayed, piled, stacked, and boxed in Roy's room.

When Roy meets someone new, he is quick to give out one of his horse business cards, and his eyes light up if he is lucky enough to meet someone who will give him a card in return. The new card will be immediately stowed safely in Roy's wallet, soon to join the ever-growing collection of Irwin Relics at home.

But despite Roy's continuous additions, the collection generally doesn't reach hoarder status, since every few years he decides to reduce the mass of the Irwin Relics cluttering his room, and he will box up some of the magazines. They aren't thrown away, of course, since they are treasures; instead, Roy donates them. He loves to support the Winters Friends of the Library and often buys books from them or donates magazines to them. I myself have owned several copies of each of the *Lord of the Rings* books, presents from Roy that he bought from the Friends of the Library book sale. I kept a single set of the paperback copies from Roy, so I can read the books without carrying around my leather-bound or illustrated editions, and the extras I share with my cousins or friends who are interested in reading them. Books aren't the only thing Roy buys at the sale, however; one time, Roy returned home with the box of *National Geographic* magazines that he had donated the prior week. After a few days of donor's remorse, Roy happily paid for the return of his Relics and returned them to their rightful spot in his collection.

Roy finally called in reinforcements to help organize his room, and Mom agreed to help him downsize the Irwin Relics. When she entered his bedroom, she was aghast. Nothing had prepared her for the decades' worth of collected souvenirs that filled every bookshelf, covered every furniture top, and hid a large percentage of the floor in Roy's room. Together they started wading through the mass, boxing up things that Roy was finally able to part with and organizing what he wanted to keep. Several boxes of magazines were loaded in the truck, ready to be donated to places in Vacaville, where Roy couldn't buy them back later. Some went to retirement centers, while others went to the Yellow Brick Road, a nonprofit organization for people with special needs, which since then has unfortunately gone out of business.

The Yellow Brick Road employed special-needs people, giving them small crafts to work on that were then sold in the store. It gave them a chance to make a living in a supportive work environment. Mom always bought handmade Christmas ornaments from the store. They were simple yet beautiful—hanging candlesticks and Christmas trees made of colorful beads and pipe cleaners.

When Mom and Roy brought magazines to the Yellow Brick Road to donate for the employees, they had to carry the boxes through the back room, where people were working on their craft projects. Mom felt uncomfortable and out of her element as they walked past the people working. Most of them had physical indications of a mental disability, such as the hallmark signs of Down Syndrome, and like most people, Mom wasn't sure how to react and interact with them and so kept quiet. In turn, they ignored Mom and continued working.

Roy had fallen behind, moving at his usual slow pace, and when he entered the room it was a completely different story. He didn't sneak through quickly and quietly like Mom had; instead, he greeted the workers, smiling and giving everyone a handshake. In return, they lit up. Smiles wreathed every face, and they happily showed Roy what they were working on. They welcomed him, not because he had a speech impediment or a learning disability, but because he showed genuine love and interest in meeting them.

"That was amazing how everyone responded to you, Roy," Mom said once they were back in the privacy of the truck. "It was like everyone came alive talking to you."

"People have always treated me differently because of how I talk," Roy said. "And there's been many times that I've wished that I could be normal. People know when you don't treat them like they're normal. Everyone wants to be treated like a person, not like they are strange or different."

That story stayed with me when I moved to San Diego and began my college career at Point Loma Nazarene University. The landscape of San Diego was almost completely opposite of what I'd known my entire life at Red Tail Farm: the irrigated, flat green farm fields were replaced by dry hills that were blanketed by buildings and scrubby brown brush. The endless asphalt roads were packed with cars, and the sidewalks were filled with people and lined with palm trees. Ironically, the hallmark palm trees were not even native species to the San Diego area, and were imported from growers, many of which were located in the far-less-tropical Northern California.

I was used to a horizon unbroken by skyscrapers and nearly devoid of people, and I always started to feel trapped after spending a few days surrounded by the metal and concrete of a big city. But at Point Loma, the claustrophobia was kept at bay by the Pacific Ocean, which commanded a hundred-and-eighty-degree view from the campus and stretched in a wide, open expanse farther than the eye could see. In its own way, it was similar to the miles of row-crop land surrounding Red Tail Farm, although the face of the ocean was constantly changing, from the steel gray and rolling whitecaps during a rare storm to the stunning flat azure of the countless sunny days. Half of the dorm rooms on campus featured a view of the ocean, and while I was assigned a room with a less-than-spectacular view of the parking lot my freshman year, being able to watch sailboats float by while enduring history class definitely helped make up for it. Luckily, for my remaining years in college I was able to obtain a bedroom with a beautifully scenic ocean view.

Although most people prefer the sunny side of San Diego, my favorite days were when the fog rolled in. Since the campus was situated on the side of a steeply sloping hill, the incoming fog was usually much lower than the structures of Point Loma, and once the billowing white clouds reached the junction of land and sea, it was easy to imagine that the school was on an island floating in the sky. Even when the fog crept up the hillside, masking the sun and filling the air with mist, I loved it. In my opinion, it was the perfect temperature—cool but not frigid—and the magical sensation begun by the illusion of a sky-island remained as buildings and trees seemed to materialize out of nothing as I walked to class.

Since Point Loma Nazarene University was a Christian college, students were mandated to attend chapel services, which were held on Monday, Wednesday, and Friday each week. It wasn't necessary to go to all of the chapel sessions, but students had to scan their student identification cards as they entered and exited in order to keep track of their chapel attendance. Each student was allotted a certain number of permissible misses, which increased each year, giving seniors the most freedom from chapel.

It was during chapel that I learned about the wide range of outreach ministries on the campus, from feeding the homeless to visiting nursing homes. A couple of the ministries were focused on helping people with special needs. One of those was called Special Friends and was run by one of my high school friends, Meredith. Together with my roommate, Amanda, I joined this ministry my third year of college.

One of the reasons that we signed up for the Special Friends ministry together was our experience volunteering at the Special Olympics during our freshman year. When she was younger, Amanda had been a member of the Mother Goose Club, which historically helped out with the annual Special Olympics in nearby Santee. Even though Amanda was no longer officially part of Mother Goose when she was in college, her friends in the organization invited her to volunteer, and she in turn invited me.

We pulled into the packed high school parking lot early Saturday morning, surprised at the overwhelming number of volunteers streaming toward the entrance to the football field and track. We quickly joined the throng, searching for Amanda's friends amongst the filled bleachers. When we found them, we learned that we were going to be assigned to help one of the athletes throughout the day. Since there were far more volunteers that day than the organizing committee was expecting, we were able to stay together and assist a single competitor.

The woman that we helped was part of a group home, with one caregiver assigned to three of the women. Together with the rest of the other young ladies from the Mother Goose organization, we were supposed to help the three women athletes get to each of their events. In reality, however, they didn't need our help, so we were able to spend the day socializing with them and cheering them on as they ran their individual races.

It was a rewarding experience to be able to meet and support athletes that are often largely ignored or overlooked by society, but at the same time it also pushed me out of my comfort zone. As with many people, it has always been easier to make friends with people who have many similarities to me, and more challenging to closely relate to someone with a drastically different background or culture. But from Roy, I've learned that it is possible to transcend the barriers that society claims divide us.

Although children in today's society aren't locked up in abusive institutions the way that Roy was as a boy, in a way they are still hidden from mainstream society, through special education classes and unfair ostracism from their peers. It is a part of our culture that needs to change. As Roy said, people know when you treat them differently than you treat others, even if they hide the pain caused by that disdain and condescension.

I kept Roy's words in mind as I joined the Special Friends ministry. One of the first events I volunteered to help at was a bowling league for teens and young adults with disabilities. On the team I was assigned to help, I met a remarkable young woman. Philina was confined to a wheelchair and was only able to bowl by pushing her ball down a ramp that was set up for her by her round-the-clock caregiver. She couldn't speak, but that didn't prevent her from being able to express her feelings through her wide smile when her ball knocked over some pins. And despite being mute, she was still able to converse, as she was fluent in American Sign Language. I didn't know a single gesture of sign language, but while I helped her to bowl, she taught me to communicate her way.

Philina's caregiver knew sign language as well, but was clearly overwhelmed by the daily task of caring for a full house of special needs young adults, including my new friend. The other three members of Philina's bowling team lived in the same household and were under the supervision of the same woman, and the caregiver had her hands full with overseeing the other bowlers. Although she interpreted a few signs for me when I got completely lost—such as telling me that Philina was singing "Itsy Bitsy Spider" to me—for the most part, I was left on my own to understand what Philina was telling me.

Philina was remarkably proficient at making her point, although occasionally she grew frustrated with my inability to engage in a two-way conversation. After an hour of bowling, Philina pointed at herself, pointed at me, and then curled her two index fingers around each other. When my brow furrowed in confusion, she repeated the gestures, and when I hesitantly mimicked her interlocked fingers, her face split in a huge smile. I may not have been fluent in sign language, but her meaning was clear: "You are my friend."

Philina next held up her hands as if holding a camera, moving her right index finger like she was taking a picture. When I asked, "Do you want me to take a picture with my cell phone?" I was rewarded with another beaming smile. I pulled out my flip-phone to take a picture of her, but she shook her head and gestured for me to come next to her and be in the picture. When I sat next to her, she put her arm around my shoulder and pulled me close for the selfie. I took several pictures of us together, and Philina beamed as she looked at them on the tiny screen of my phone. When she was done admiring the pictures, she returned my phone to me and made the gesture of friendship. As with many instances in life, I came into a situation expecting to be the one dispensing help, and instead I was humbled and placed in the role of student.

After volunteering at the Special Olympics and then meeting Philina at the bowling alley, I thought I knew what to expect when Meredith, the leader of Special Friends, announced that the next event would be attending a wheelchair basketball game. Once again, however, my expectations fell far short of reality.

I knew that the athletes would be physically disabled, but I had made the incorrect assumption that they would also be intellectually disabled, like the competitors of the Special Olympics. Based on my experience at the Special Olympics, I thought we would be helping out and cheering on the teams.

Instead, I was introduced to the sport of quad rugby, where men and women in armored wheelchairs, reminiscent of Roman battle chariots, fiercely competed in an intense, high-contact sport. It quickly became obvious why the sport was originally dubbed "Murderball," as the heavily reinforced wheelchairs slammed into one another, players jockeying for position and fighting for the volleyball that was used as the game ball. More than one player's wheelchair was flipped over during the course of the game, and many of the athletes were able to right themselves without a pause, like watching a whitewater kayaker execute rolls in the water. It was quickly apparent that we were not at the event as helpers; we were spectators, and we settled in the stands to watch and cheer for athletes competing on a near-professional level.

Even when athletes had blowouts of their wheelchair tires there was barely a pause in the flow of the game. The coaches, who for the most part were able-bodied, would rush onto the court and change the athlete's tire; the speed was akin to watching the pit crew at a NASCAR race. As soon as they finished, the referees would blow their whistles and the game would resume.

The event that had the most profound impact on me, however, was a picnic hosted by the San Diego Parks and Recreation at Crown Point on

Mission Bay. It was there that I met Zane, a young man my age who had Asperger Syndrome. Zane reminded me of a young Roy—bitter and resentful that people treated him differently than others, wishing that he could be normal. It was clear that he, like Roy, was caught between two worlds; he wasn't disabled to the point that he couldn't function in society, but he was different enough from most people that many of them rejected him simply because of that difference. Zane knew that, and he hated it.

When I first saw him, he was challenging another girl from Point Loma on her reasons for volunteering to help. "I've seen this my whole life with people helping at Parks and Rec. You come to events and act like you like us, but none of you actually wants to be friends with us. You just come here to make yourselves feel better, like 'Hey, I helped someone less fortunate than me today.' But that's all it is, a selfish act. Nobody wants to hang out after an event or do something else. Suddenly they're busy and want to spend time with their real friends."

The girl he was speaking to was clearly flustered, unsure how to respond to the attack. I realized that both of us could see the truth in Zane's words.

"That's not true!" she protested.

"Isn't it? Do you ever spend any time with anyone here, besides your friends from school, outside of your volunteer events? It's the same thing as everyone else I've seen. You just do this to look good."

I stepped in to rescue the girl, who was speechless after the onslaught. "That's not entirely true. I have a good friend back home with a learning disability. His name is Roy. I've known him for years. And I don't spend time with him out of pity or because it makes me look good. He's a great guy. Everyone in my town loves him."

"So does that mean you'd want to hang out sometime?" Zane challenged.

I was a little leery; after all, I didn't know him at all. But it didn't seem like a ploy to spend time with a girl; there was genuine hurt, anger, and doubt written plainly across his face.

"Depends on what we did," I said.

"If I give you my number, you're going to just forget about me once you get back to school," Zane said. "You'll think of excuses not to hang out with me."

"No, I won't," I replied. "I mean what I say."

Disbelief was still written on Zane's face after we exchanged phone numbers and I climbed in the van with my other friends and headed back to school. Just like Roy as a child, life hadn't been easy or fair to Zane.

To Zane's surprise, I responded to his text messages, and before long we were spending time together, and it wasn't because I felt sorry for him or wanted to prove that he was wrong. I had genuine fun with him, going on extraordinary adventures to places in San Diego County that I would otherwise not have known about, from eating at a hole-in-the-wall Ethiopian restaurant to visiting the Palomar Observatory high in the mountains.

Zane had a passion for trains, so we went to the Pacific Southwest Railway Museum in Campo and wandered amongst the antique engines and train cars sitting on the tracks. The museum offered train rides on certain weekends, but our trip was spur-of-the-moment and we hadn't thought to check the schedule to see if the trains were running that weekend. They weren't.

Another weekend, Zane and I visited Rohr Park, a public park in Chula Vista that had small train tracks, where train hobbyists would bring their locomotives on the weekends to ride around the park and share their trains with children. Zane had often ridden on the pint-sized railways as a child, but the only things on the tracks that day were our feet as we walked along the rails like balance beams.

It was a friendship that neither of us expected to form that day at the picnic, but it was one that strengthened both of us, as all good friendships do. If it hadn't been for knowing Roy, and seeing how he effortlessly interacts with people from all walks of life, I never would have met Zane. Even after I graduated from Point Loma and moved away, our friendship continued. From then on, whenever I visited San Diego, I always made sure to give Zane a call and find out what adventure was next on the schedule.

Chapter 17
Roy Returns

IN THE SUMMER of 2009, Steve and Roy returned to Michigan for the first time in two and a half decades. The first thing they did upon their arrival was visit the property that Roy had known as the Lapeer State Home and Training School, the place where he was institutionalized for four years. The memories from that wretched place had haunted him his entire life, and Roy was ready to face the ghosts of his past and leave them behind him once and for all.

What had begun as The Michigan Home for the Feeble-Minded and Epileptic in 1895 was no longer recognizable. The place of oppression and abuse had changed its name several times over the course of nearly a hundred years, and although the methods of treating its residents had slowly advanced over time, the bleak institution had always remained a place to send the outcasts of society where they would be out of sight and out of mind. The number of residents at the institution had declined in the years following Roy's internment, until finally it was no longer financially sustainable to remain open. The doors of the institution were closed forever in 1991. After its closure, all but two of the institution's buildings had been razed to the ground.

But the property itself wasn't abandoned. New edifices sprung up to replace the old buildings, ready to shape a new group of young adults. And just as the structures covering the property changed, so did its purpose. When Roy had been an illiterate and stuttering teenaged boy, he had spent the worst years of his life at the institution, but now the land was dedicated to providing what had been denied to the previous occupants: an education.

Mott Community College had purchased the land, turning it into the campus for their Lapeer Extension. Roy walked the grounds of the school, peace washing over him as he watched young adults of all backgrounds taking advantage of the learning opportunities that he had been denied. He wasn't jealous of them; rather, he was proud of the students and overjoyed that the very place where he had been beaten down was now being used to lift people up.

After making his peace at the place that formed the most negative memories of his life, Roy returned to the place that was the most positively influential on him as a young man: the Grosse Pointe Hunt Club. The four years he spent working there were sharply etched in his memory, although it had been a quarter of a century since he had set foot on the property. The old clubhouse where Roy would get hamburgers and coffee was still there, as was the indoor riding arena where Roy rode for the first time.

But the old stable, where Roy walked his rounds and gave carrots to the horses, was gone. It had burned to the ground in 2001, when a man threw a firecracker into the barn in order to scare the horses. The dry wood building caught fire with twenty-four horses trapped within, hay and wood shavings spreading the blaze at an astronomical rate. The lone night watchman was only able to save five of his charges before the inferno drove him out, leaving the other horses to suffer horrific deaths in the smoke and flames.

Roy had heard of the tragedy when it happened, as he still kept in contact with old friends from the hunt club, but seeing the new barn was a dagger to the heart, a reminder of the nineteen lives lost in a place that had once been under his guardianship. But the new stable was beautiful, an elegant green-and-white structure with a horseshoe-shaped floor plan, and it had been built with particular care so the tragedy would not repeat itself. Instead of each stall having a single door that led to the center aisle of the barn, as is common in many stables, the stalls were constructed with two doors, one in the aisle and one on the outside of the barn, so the horses could be set loose through the outer gates in the event of another fire.

Roy took a bag of carrots to feed the residents of the new barn. When he walked up to the first stall, none of the horses were visible. But at the sound of the first carrot snapping, a dozen equines poked their heads out of their gates, ears perked forward in anticipation of a treat. Roy walked down the row, handing carrot pieces to each horse and murmuring, "Good horse," until he neared the end. A dark bay had its ears pinned, glaring at its neighbors as it stretched its nose toward Roy.

"Get your ears up!" Roy commanded. The horse tossed its head and tried to grab for a carrot. "No! Get your ears up!" he ordered, keeping out of range of the cantankerous animal.

The horse's fierce glare didn't abate, so Roy moved on to the next horse without giving it any carrots. "I don't trust them when their ears are back," he told Steve. "They'll bite."

After doling out the treats, Roy and Steve returned to the Brownells' home, which sat on property that bordered the pastures of the hunt club, easily accessed by a small gate in the pasture's wood-railed fencing. For the duration of their trip, the Irwin brothers stayed with the Brownells, who were the daughter and son-in-law of Jack Kirlin, a member of the hunt club at the time Roy was night watchman. Roy and Kirlin stayed in contact over the years, exchanging phone calls and Christmas cards.

At the rear of the massive home was an in-law suite, originally built for the Kirlins, but it had never served its intended purpose. It was perfect guest quarters for the Irwin brothers, and Roy could sit in the living room and watch horses graze in the pastures of the hunt club, sipping a blue pop from the ample stock in the fridge.

The next day, the Irwins toured the massive Edsel and Eleanor Ford Estate, which had been built in 1929 and was the residence of the reigning heirs to Henry Ford's empire when Roy and Steve were growing up. To young Steve, the gated and walled complex had been an ominous mystery, something to marvel at while riding past on a bicycle but unapproachable and foreign.

But Roy wasn't frightened off by the massive stone wall, complete with iron gate and occupied guardhouse. When Roy was twelve, he walked to the estate one day and saw a man cleaning the concrete sidewalk in front of the gate.

"Hi, my name is Roy," he said, with the outspoken sociability he has had his entire life.

"I'm Thomas Laughlin," the man replied. "You can call me Tommy."

Roy quickly fell into conversation with the man, who was about sixty years old and pleasantly surprised by being approached by the boy wandering down the street. Tommy told Roy his life story: Born in Ireland, he moved to the US and began working in the Ford factory. After a while, he became Henry Ford's personal chauffeur, and then later a bodyguard and head of security for Henry's son, Edsel Ford. Roy was fascinated to hear about Tommy's experience as a boxer, which had helped Tommy secure the position of bodyguard.

Before he left, Roy asked if he could look at the massive mansion hidden behind the tall stone wall. Tommy smiled. "Sure," he said. He opened the gate and walked through, then turned and was surprised to see Roy still standing on the sidewalk, out of sight of the manor. "Aren't you going to come in?"

"I wanted to wait until I was invited," Roy replied.

Tommy's grin expanded to split his face in two. "Come on in, Roy."

Roy walked through the archway of the gate, his eyes widening as he took in the splendor of the sixty-room stone mansion. He thanked Tommy for trusting him to come inside the gate and then headed home.

As Roy grew up, he retained his friendship with Tommy, who was always kind to Roy and happy to share stories of his life with the boy. Their friendship came to an end when the Irwin family left Michigan and moved to California, and by the time the brothers returned, Tommy had been gone for years. He passed away in 1972, after a remarkable fifty-six-year-long career in the employ of the Fords.

The Irwin brothers had chosen the time of their visit to Michigan to coincide with the Grosse Pointe Hunt Club's annual summer show, and the following day, they reclined in the shade of a temporary canopy while they watched the competition. Over a hundred and forty riders had entered the show, some traveling hundreds of miles for the event. As trailer after trailer had entered the grounds in the days preceding the show, Roy laughed as he recalled Mom pulling her own horse trailer; when backing up, she always turned off the radio and demanded absolute silence from her passengers. Roy knew this, and liked to tease her about it. His favorite reaction was when she would threaten to make him walk home if he wasn't quiet.

Other memories, memories of his time at the hunt club, played through Roy's mind as the show finally commenced. Some were bitter, like the recollection of a group of men who turned their backs on Roy and left the room when he asked how they were doing. Others made him laugh as he recounted them to Steve.

"The riding arena was for when kids learned how to jump," Roy said. "And one day, I was watching a girl taking a lesson, and when they came up to a jump, the horse went one way and she went the other!"

During the show, however, horses and riders worked together in a harmonious partnership. Roy's heart soared as he watched the horses sail over the jumps, gracefully clearing the poles and fences. A fire rekindled in his heart, and he decided that one day, he too would master the art of riding one of those magnificent creatures.

Chapter 18
Dreams Fulfilled

AS I CONTINUED college, I finally received the opportunity to fulfill a wish that I'd had for years: breed Cassie in order to continue her bloodline, so that I could have her offspring to ride when Cassie got older. California was fairly devoid of Fox Trotter stallions, but twenty miles from my grandparents' home in Colorado was a magnificent stallion, an amber champagne named Dusty's Smoke.

Mom and I took Cassie, Duchess, and Rain Dance to Colorado the summer before my second year of college. They stayed at the ranch near my grandparent's house, and my grandma drove over once a month to take them to the vet for a pregnancy check. I had planned on helping Mom bring the mares back, but the horses had their own schedule, and it wasn't until I was back in school that Grandma sent us an email with the pictures we had been long expecting: three blurry black-and-gray ultrasound images that were the embryos.

But Grandma's email also contained bad news: all three of the mares had been gradually losing weight over the summer, which Grandma hadn't noticed at first, but now it was unmistakable, as their ribs were beginning to show under their coats. Apparently the ranch owner had been using the money we paid her for daily feed to buy hay for her own horses instead. Grandma called one of her friends, who offered to care for our horses at her own ranch until Mom was able to fetch them in the middle of September.

Like an overeager expectant parent, I printed off the ultrasound pictures of all three mares' embryos, scribbled the due dates of each at the bottom, and taped them to my dorm room wall. My roommate, Amanda, laughed at my excitement over the three indiscernible blobs, but I couldn't wait for the foals to finally arrive.

Horses are pregnant for eleven months, so it wasn't until the beginning of June that the first foal was due, a month after I returned home for the summer. By then, the mares had more than recovered from their ordeal in Colorado. All three were fat and healthy, clearly enjoying the extra feed that they received due to their pregnancies. But as the due dates drew nearer, it became more apparent that they might only be fat, rather than pregnant. First Rain Dance, then Duchess, passed their due dates with no signs of an impending baby: their hips didn't change, their bellies didn't bulge and sag, they produced no milk, and finally we had to admit that they weren't pregnant. The partial starvation followed by a long trailer journey had clearly proven too stressful on their bodies, and at some point they reabsorbed the developing fetuses.

Our last hope was Cassie, who wasn't due until the beginning of July. But unlike the other two mares, Cassie's pendulous belly made it perfectly clear that she hadn't succumbed to the stress like they had. As her due date approached, I set up the foaling stall with a thick bed of straw and prepared a foaling kit to have on hand—antiseptic to sterilize the newborn's umbilical stump, a stack of clean towels to dry the foal, disposable surgical gloves, an enema in case the foal struggled too much to pass meconium, and a large trash bag for collecting the placenta.

A few days before Cassie was due, I moved her to the foaling stall and Mom parked the motorhome next to the fence so we could spend the night at the barn and listen for Cassie's water to break. A couple times a day, I examined Cassie to see how she was progressing. Her udder was full and her hindquarters had softened in preparation for the birth. When I picked up her tail, which normally had moderate resistance, it was limp like a dishrag.

"I'm ninety-nine percent sure it won't be tonight, and fifty percent sure it won't be the next night," I predicted. "I think she's going to have it on the third night."

"Still, we should sleep at the barn anyway. We don't want to miss it," Mom replied.

"Yes, I know."

The next day, there was still no baby, although Cassie's udder waxed up, as colostrum slowly dripped out and formed stalactites on her teats.

"It might be tonight, but I think it will be tomorrow," I said.

"I think you're right, but she's looking pretty close," Mom said.

By the next morning, milk was running down Cassie's back legs and she was clearly uncomfortable, turning her head around to bite her sides and swishing her tail in annoyance. Mom and I knew for certain that the foal was going to be born that night.

I was restless all day, checking on Cassie frequently to make sure she wasn't going to have a daytime birth, which is unusual but not unheard-of for horses. I couldn't wait to see the baby; I had wanted to have a foal from Cassie for years. Although I hoped it would be a champagne, I was more focused on the gender of the foal—more than anything, I wanted a filly, because I could breed a filly in the future and continue the bloodline, but a colt would have to be gelded and would become a genetic dead end.

That evening, I watched a movie to pass the time before going to the barn to sleep. At nine o'clock, while the movie was still playing, Mom and Dad decided to go to the barn to get ice cream from the freezer in the tack room. Five minutes later, my cell phone rang.

"Get out here now! Cassie's having the baby!"

I bolted up from the couch and raced to the barn, not even taking the time to zip up my paddock boots. When I arrived, Cassie was flat on her side, a pair of tiny hooves visible at her back end. Mom and I quietly entered the stall to assist her. Soon a head emerged, and as Mom cleared away the sack from the foal's face, it opened its eyes and looked around, curious about this strange new world. Its eyes were brown, rather than hallmark blue of a newborn champagne, and its coat was a dark red. A bright white star with a long thin stripe ran down its chestnut head.

After a few more minutes of Cassie pushing, the rest of the foal emerged. I toweled it dry as Mom checked between its legs.

"It's a girl," Mom said.

"Yes!" I exulted, until Mom took another look.

"Nope, I was wrong. It's a colt. A chestnut colt."

Disappointment washed through me. "That's okay, pretty baby," I crooned. "You're just going to have to get a little sister sometime."

Although I only got to spend a month with the colt before I returned to school, I made that month count. I began riding Cassie again, staying in the alfalfa field surrounding our house and letting the colt run free and follow Cassie at will. Soon it became apparent that he had his mother's competitive drive. He sprinted ahead of her when they were loose in the pasture together, forcing her to chase after him, and he reveled in the freedom of running by her side when I took her out for a gallop. Soon I decided on a name for him: Wind Racer.

But before long, I had to say goodbye to Racer and fly back down to San Diego for my third and final year of college. I looked forward to each break from school, since it meant I could spend some time with my colt, who was about a hundred pounds heavier each time I saw him. At last, it was the end of the school year, and time for me to leave San Diego for good.

I graduated from Point Loma Nazarene University in May of 2010, completing a bachelor's degree in Writing with a minor in Biology. I moved home and began to write, supporting this endeavor by training and riding a few horses, ranch-sitting (taking care of ranches while the owners were away, feeding and caring for everything from cats and dogs to cows and goats), and taking care of Red Tail Farm in exchange for room and board for both me and my horses.

That first summer included another task: Roy decided that he wanted to restart his riding lessons and learn how to ride well enough to give a riding demonstration to his friends on his birthday, just as he had done the round pen training demonstration eight years earlier.

For his mount, Mom and I chose Rokko, Cassie's younger brother, who had finally grown from a gangly, awkward colt to a tall, sleek gelding. Rokko had become Red Tail Farm's beginner-level horse, as he had the same easygoing, laid-back personality of Cassie, without the readiness she had to accelerate like a Ferrari. Whenever a green rider was set atop Rokko and let loose in the arena, the gentle giant happily plodded around the sandy enclosure at a sedate walk, his only vice his tendency to seek out every weed patch and stop for a nibble while the rider futilely pulled on the reins and kicked his sides in an effort to get him to continue moving.

When his handler was on the ground, Rokko could be a little more ornery. He knew he could get away with things with beginners, and would use them as a scratching post to rub his itchy, sweaty face at the end of a ride, earning him the nickname "Pest." Despite this annoyance, since the passing of Damien and the sale of Rowdy, Rokko was the safest horse under saddle for a beginner. He never bucked or bolted, and he had a whole lot more "whoa than go." Rather than trying to take over and run back to the barn like some horses do with beginners while on the trail, Rokko would stop for a snack instead, which, while frustrating for the beginner learning to control the horse, was not frightening like a horse trying to go faster.

When Jenna was younger and first learning to ride, she had been the first beginner rider to be placed on Rokko, the year after Damien passed away. Jenna was eleven and Rokko was only four, an exceptionally young age for a horse to be trusted with a green rider.

Despite this, Mom and I knew he would be the perfect horse for Jenna—not because he was a perfect horse, but because his flaws would help build her into a better, more confident rider. Jenna was always quiet, shy, and devoid of an authoritative manner. With Rokko, a rider with a timid attitude would never get anywhere, because Rokko would just spend the whole time grazing instead of working. Jenna had to develop confidence and a commanding attitude if she wanted to have fun riding him.

After a few days of riding at Red Tail Farm, Mom and I took Jenna to Point Reyes National Seashore and rode down the Bear Valley Trail to the ocean, one of our favorite rides. At the end of the trail, we stopped on the top of a cliff overlooking the beautiful Pacific Ocean and had lunch.

Unfortunately for Jenna, there was no place for us to tie our horses while we ate, so we held onto their lead ropes and let them nibble on grass while we consumed our sandwiches. I even sat on the ground and leisurely ate while Cassie grazed in a circle around me. Mom, with Duke, also had no problems with her horse standing quietly while she finished her meal.

Jenna, on the other hand, had the Pest to deal with. Rokko wasn't satisfied with the dried, scrubby grass of the coast, and he dragged Jenna around us in a search for better fodder. When the sweaty skin under his bridle annoyed him, Rokko knocked Jenna off-balance by rubbing the itchy spots behind his ears on her shoulder. In a move that Jenna probably saw as cruel, Mom and I didn't rescue her. We gave her advice but let her deal with Rokko herself, forcing her to assert herself and command the horse, and by the end of our lunch she was successful in getting Rokko to obey.

The summers of dealing with Rokko the Pest ended up being incredibly beneficial for Jenna. He helped her blossom into a remarkable, confident young woman. By the time she met her future horse, Jagger, she was ready and unafraid to face the challenge of the feisty young Arabian-Saddlebred cross.

By the time Roy decided to learn to ride, Rokko had fortunately retained his good qualities and been trained out of most of his bad habits. Roy was also experienced and assertive enough to not allow Rokko to use him as a rubbing post.

Roy only had a month and a half to prepare before his birthday, so a few times a week Mom or I drove to town and brought Roy back to Red Tail Farm for a riding lesson. We set up a few obstacles in the arena for Roy to work on controlling the horse's direction: a line of cones for them to weave through, a row of poles laid on the ground for them to step over, and an L-shaped path made out of poles, which required the horse to make a sharp ninety-degree turn while remaining within the pole "barrier." We told Roy to imagine that it was a bridge, and if the horse stepped over the poles, they "fell" and perished in the imaginary chasm on either side.

At first, Rokko wouldn't make a tight enough turn, and one hoof would land off the "bridge," or he would be slow to bend in the opposite direction when weaving through the cones and some of the cones would get skipped. But Roy started figuring out how to control the horse from the saddle, telling Rokko where to go with a soft but firm hand as he urged Rokko on with commands of, "Come on, boy, let's go!"

Rokko ignored Roy's urging to go faster at first, plodding along in his typical sedate walk, his head low and his body relaxed. As he started to accept Roy's authority from the reins, however, he decided to listen to Roy's spoken command, "Let's go!" The second week of their lessons together, Rokko's ears perked up when Roy urged him forward, and he gently accelerated into a lumbering canter across the arena, Roy clinging to the horn of his saddle in shock.

From my vantage point outside the arena, my heart stopped as Rokko happily cantered—which to Roy undoubtedly felt like the surging charge of Secretariat racing for the finish line during the Belmont Stakes—and I bolted into the arena, praying that Roy would stay on and that Rokko wouldn't unseat him by making a sharp turn or sudden stop at the end of the arena, since they were headed down the center of the oval directly toward the end fence, rather than along the gentle curve of the outside rail.

But Roy managed to keep his grip on the reins, and he pulled back, telling Rokko to stop. Rokko obliged, licking his lips in contentment as he slowed down and came to a smooth stop. I hurried to Rokko's side to check on Roy, who was still wide-eyed and breathless from the unexpected run.

"He just started running! Why did he do that?" Roy asked.

"Well, Roy, you've been asking him to go faster the whole time you've been riding him," I replied. "I guess he finally decided you meant it. So for now on, don't tell him to go faster when he's walking, since that's what you want him to do and he's doing what you are asking."

"Okay," Roy said. "Can I get off now?"

"How about you do one more lap around the arena at a walk, so that you end on a good note," I said. "That's always important when you're working with a horse."

Roy finished his ride, keeping quiet while Rokko walked sedately around the arena, then climbed down from the saddle on shaky legs. The fright wasn't enough to deter him, however, and he continued to take lessons in preparation for his riding demonstration.

Chapter 19
Birthday Bucking

JULY 6, 2010, Roy's seventy-second birthday, dawned cloudless and warm. It was the perfect weather for riding, the sun shining but without the intensity and vengeance of a true summer day. Everything was set for success: Mom was busy preparing buffet-style food, Roy was getting a ride to the ranch from Steve, and Rokko was a sleek and shining black from his bath the day before. I thought it was going to be just another day of Roy riding Rokko—a final, easy ride, since Roy had decided that this demonstration was going to be his last time in the saddle.

That was before I went to the barn.

Rokko fidgeted as I brushed and tacked him, moving from side to side and attempting to gnaw on the lead rope every time my back was turned, but that was fairly typical for the class clown of the barn. He sidled away from me as I tightened the cinch on Roy's saddle, tossed his head as I put on the bridle, and then stood chomping on the bit.

I grabbed my helmet and led Rokko out to the arena, intending to give him a bit of a warm-up before we heaved Roy into the saddle.

The moment I swung into the saddle, I knew something was wrong. The normally placid and somewhat lazy horse was tense, ready to move. When I asked him to walk, he frisked, pulling at the bit and trying to speed up.

"Easy boy," I murmured, stroking his sleek, arched neck and holding him at a walk.

After a lap around the arena I decided to let him trot in order to release some of his pent-up energy. Normally Rokko lumbered across the turf, weight shifted forward on his front end, his feet pounding the ground in a slow clip. Not today.

He moved immediately into a rapid foxtrot, his head up and his feet gliding across the ground like Pegasus about to take flight. With the grace of a ballerina he danced around the arena, his weight thrown back on his powerful, driving hindquarters, his head straining against the reins as he sought to break into a run.

I held him in the foxtrot for a few laps, letting his muscles warm up. Then I shifted my weight slightly, tightening my knees as I let a little slack in the reins.

Immediately Rokko made a flawless transition into a gallop, his long legs eating up the ground as he continued to nearly soar above the earth.

After a half-dozen laps, usually more than enough to tire him out and make him beg to walk, I gently pulled on the reins, asking him to slow. He chomped anxiously on the bit as I increased the pressure, making him prance to a stop.

"What's the matter with you today, Rokko boy?" I asked, petting his neck to try and soothe him.

He tossed his head, prancing sideways.

"Whoa, buddy," I commanded, tapping his side with my leg to halt the movement. "Maybe I'll let you run around for a bit."

As I swung back to the ground, I saw the first car making its way down the gravel driveway. It was almost time for the party to start. I unclipped the reins and stepped back from Rokko's head.

"Go on, boy," I said, swinging the reins in a circle to tell him to move away from me.

With a powerful push he spun away from me, hooves digging into the sand in an immediate gallop. He raced a few strides before dropping his head and rounding out his back like a rodeo bronco, throwing his back legs into the air in one huge buck after another.

I muttered a few choice words as I saw more cars coming down the driveway, while Rokko continued his high-speed bucking rampage around the arena.

After several laps Rokko finally ceased bucking and slowed from a gallop, prancing with his head high as he snorted and blew, before turning to the center of the arena and trotting up to me.

The final car rolled up to the house as Rokko stopped before me. I reached up and rubbed his forehead, peering into his eyes to see if he had calmed down. He tilted his head and pushed it toward me, like a dog that wanted its ears scratched. I rubbed the sweaty spot where the bridle rested behind his ears and he finally dropped his head, letting out a big sigh of contentment.

I clipped the reins back on his bit and stepped to his shoulder, laying my hand on his warm neck. He seemed more relaxed, but could I trust him to keep Roy safe? Or would he want to prance and run? I saw the guests gather outside the house, ready to walk out to the barn, and knew I was out of time.

"God," I prayed fervently in a whisper, my hand resting on Rokko's neck. "You created all the creatures of the earth. You kept the lions from eating Daniel and made the ass speak to Balaam. You alone have the power to control all animals. Please, Lord, help me now. Keep this horse calm and relaxed. Let Roy stay safe as he rides today. Let this be a day of rejoicing and celebration, with no problems or mishaps. In the name of your Son, Jesus Christ, Amen."

I led Rokko back into the barn and tied him up. Roy, Mom, and the guests entered the barn as I finished shortening the stirrups on the saddle so they would fit Roy.

"Happy birthday, Roy," I said, smiling and giving Roy a hug, and gave a wave of hello to the others.

"This is Rokko," Mom said to the guests in introduction as Roy gave the black horse a pat. "He is an eight-year-old Missouri Fox Trotting horse, and Roy has been practicing for the last couple months with him to give you a little riding demonstration." A murmur of appreciation swept through the small group. "Now, if you'll follow me, we can go out to the arena to watch."

I led Rokko slowly behind the crowd, heart pounding. He held his head low, his muscles relaxed, seemingly at ease, but I couldn't help but feel a decided sense of unease as I checked his cinch for the last time, tightening it a few notches.

I halted him next to the mounting block, holding my hand against his side to keep him from stepping away from it while Roy climbed the steps to the top. Rokko chomped the bit noisily but was otherwise still as Dad helped Roy climb into the saddle and swing his leg over to the other side. I guided his boot into the stirrup.

"Ready?" I asked.

Roy shifted his weight around to get a little more comfortable and picked up the reins.

"Okay."

I released my clammy grip on the reins and walked forward to open the arena gate.

"Come on, boy," Roy said, swinging his legs out and back to tap Rokko's sides.

The tall black gelding plodded forward into the arena, turning to the right at Roy's gentle tug on the rein to begin an ambling lap along the fence.

I sat down on the mounting block to watch, blood pumping through my veins like I'd just finished a hundred-meter dash. I kept a close eye on Rokko, ready to run out and grab his bridle at the first sign of friskiness.

Mercifully my fears proved groundless as Roy and Rokko continued their demonstration, the perfect image of man and horse in complete harmony with one another. Rokko's body gently curved at the soft touch of the rein as they wove in and out of the traffic cones. The ninety-degree turn of the pole "bridge" was tackled with ease, without a single hoof stepping over the line. Finally Roy pulled Rokko to a halt in front of the core group of the Roy Irwin Fan Club, then gave a light tug on the reins to ask Rokko to back up. Rokko lowered his head in submission and reversed in a straight line away from the small crowd.

I let out a sigh of relief as everyone applauded. The demonstration had gone better than I could have hoped, the ultimate culmination of long hours of practice and preparation. For that quarter of an hour, Roy was not merely a man on a horse; he was a horseman.

Chapter 20
Continued Inspiration

ON NOVEMBER 19, 2010, a few months after Roy's final ride on Rokko, I drove into town to pick Roy up and take him to speak to students. Roy was no longer going to schools in other towns to talk, but every year, he still went to Shirley Rominger Intermediate School in Winters and spoke in the classroom of Woody Fridae, a friend of Roy's who taught fifth grade.

As we pulled into the school parking lot at ten in the morning, I felt an eerie sense of déjà vu. I hadn't attended Shirley Rominger when I was in school; I was in the eighth grade when it was being constructed. But the campus was situated catercorner to Winters Middle School, and the year before Shirley Rominger opened, its gymnasium was used as the practice room for the middle school band. As a band member, I made the daily trek across the soccer fields to play music in the new school, where we could blare our instruments as loudly as we pleased without risking upsetting a neighboring classroom.

Roy and I entered the large blue-roofed white building that contained the gym in the center and the administration offices on the side. Everything was clean, orderly, and pristine, seemingly still smelling of wet paint. Seven years wasn't enough to give the school the degenerating, depressing feeling of many educational facilities; it was light and fresh, almost with an air of hope for the future.

I felt like I was stepping backward in time as Roy and I signed in, receiving official visitor's passes—our names written in Sharpie on rectangular name tag stickers. The secretary at the front desk was the mother of one of my former classmates. As Roy and I talked to her, the principal overheard Roy's voice and came out of her office to say hello. It was Pam Scheeline, who was my kindergarten principal. She was pivotal in developing my love of reading; when I was in kindergarten, she would take me out of class and read books with me, helping me learn how to read and passing on a love of the written word. She had also helped Roy in his reading endeavors.

We didn't have long to talk, as we were due in Mr. Fridae's class at ten thirty. We left the office and walked to his classroom, which was empty of students, who still had a few minutes of recess left. Mr. Fridae was in the room, digging through his library in a search for his copy of Roy's training DVD.

After we said hello, Mr. Fridae said to me, "You were in my class when you were in school, weren't you?"

"Yes, but it was just for math," I replied. When I was in the fifth grade, students were in a homeroom for most of the day but had a separate teacher for math and P.E. I suppose it was to help prepare us for the separated subjects and multiple teachers in middle school, but the school district had apparently abandoned that approach, as Mr. Fridae was no longer specifically a math teacher.

"Did you go to Angel Island?" Mr. Fridae asked.

"Yeah, that was a lot of fun!" I grinned as I remembered the weekend trip to Angel Island, a small hilly island set in San Francisco Bay. Every year, Mr. Fridae took a group of students there for a Civil War Reenactment. We dressed up as Union Soldiers and marched to an old barracks, where we learned fun things like how to hold a musket (non-operable, of course), make hardtack, sing battle songs, and use signal flags. At the end of the weekend, the squad that performed the best got to shoot a real cannon (minus the cannonball) toward the Golden Gate Bridge.

"We are just getting ready for our trip next spring," Mr. Fridae said, showing me a rack that had blue wool coats hanging from it. I recalled going to the Goodwill with Mom and buying my own blue coat for Angel Island. After school, the group of future Union soldiers would meet and learn how to sew red chevrons for rank and brass eagle buttons onto our secondhand coats. Our "authentic" Civil War pants were jeans with a red stripe sewn down the side of the legs.

A loud bell suddenly rang outside, signaling the end of the students' recess. They soon began streaming into the classroom, taking their seats at their small desks. When they had all entered, Mr. Fridae introduced us.

"We have some special guests with us here today. This is my good friend, Roy Irwin, who is going to talk to you. With him is Lauren Filarsky, who was one of my students back when she was your age. How long ago was that, Lauren?"

"About ten years," I said. The students looked at me with wide eyes. I suddenly felt old; all of the current students were all born around the time that I had been in Mr. Fridae's class.

"We are going to watch part of Roy's video, then listen to him speak. Make sure to pay attention and take notes, because I am going to give you a quiz later about what you learned." Mr. Fridae had one of the students turn out the lights, and we watched a few minutes of Roy working with Rowdy in the round pen. When Mr. Fridae stopped the video and the lights were turned back on, I stood up to speak. Roy had asked me to introduce him and give the students a little background about his life.

I was surprised that I was a little nervous when I started talking. Perhaps it was because Mom had always been the one to introduce Roy, and when I was present for the talks, I was always sitting in the back of the classroom. I hadn't even been to one of Roy's talks since I had been in the eighth grade; once I reached high school, I left the Winters school system, and then during college I was in San Diego when Roy did his talks.

"Hi, I'm Lauren," I said. "I've known Roy since I was about your age. When he was a kid, he wasn't given the opportunity to learn. He was institutionalized and not taught to read. When he was a young man, he worked for the Grosse Pointe Hunt Club in Michigan, where he learned to take care of horses. After he moved to Winters, he learned to read and write at the age of fifty.

"Roy started coming out to my family's ranch about ten years ago and learned how to train horses in the round pen, which you just saw. He gave a training demonstration at the Western States Horse Expo, which is the largest horse exposition in the United States. Last year, he learned how to ride, which had been his dream for a long time." I trailed off somewhat awkwardly and sat down.

Roy stepped up to the front of the classroom, took a deep breath, and began to speak. "You know, when I was your age, kids used to tease me a lot because of my speech difficulty. You might notice when I talk I kind of stammer. Well, they put me in an institution for four years because of it. My uncle was a psychologist, and he thought I could maybe learn a trade.

"I didn't know how to read, write, or do anything. Because they didn't teach me! And at the institution, the kids were mean too. One hit me with a belt buckle. And see here"—Roy rolled up the sleeve of his Red Tail Farm sweatshirt—"I still have a scar from where one guy bit me.

"When I got out, I used to go boozing all the time. I thought it was okay, but it wasn't. It just makes you unhappier."

Roy grew suddenly nostalgic, changing the topic. "My momma and daddy are dead now. And I miss them a lot. How many of you have parents?" The children raised their hands.

"You're lucky to still have them. You should ask them about their childhood. And if you write it down, then you can still have a part of them with you after they die, even when you're old, like me.

"Believe it or not, I'm seventy-two years old. I'm going to school like you, to learn numbers. When you're seventy-two, it's very hard to take this in. You have a lot of work to do to learn. Believe me, I know! It's very difficult, but you can do it."

Roy moved into his favorite topic. "Horses are my love. I went to the Hunt Club in April to get a job. It was snowing and nobody was around, but I saw a smokestack so I knew someone was there. At that time, I didn't know the front from the back of a horse. I saw all those horses and thought, 'What am I getting into?'

"I met Red LaPearl, and he gave me a job. He was a character! He liked horses better than he liked people. But he taught me about horses and I liked working for him. It got me started for when I later met Cheryl, and she showed me how to work with horses in the round pen. I never knew I could do something like that. Even my teachers told me I couldn't do anything.

"You know, you have a beautiful thing here. You have teachers who will teach you, you have a wonderful future. You are all more advanced than I am at school, but that's all right with me. I started going to school because I wanted to do my Christmas cards myself."

Roy had fulfilled that dream of doing his own Christmas cards: Every year, we receive in the mail a Christmas card with a Bible verse and Roy's looping signature inside, with a picture of a steam engine chugging through a snowy landscape on the front. Roy often picks a card with a train, because it reminds him of his boyhood summers when he would visit his grandmother, who lived across a field from a train yard. During the day, Roy would explore the train yard. The workers knew who he was and left him alone, other than to warn him to be careful when the trains were moving; besides the danger of being run over, several of the men were missing fingers from the boxcars banging into one another when they were being coupled together. One of the engineers even invited Roy and Steve, then "just a little tyke," to go for a ride one day as he moved trains around the yard. Roy was fascinated by the locomotive, learning how the train was controlled and discovering the deadman's switch, which would stop the train in the event the engineer died while it was moving. As Roy lay in bed at night, the sound of the locomotives would lull him to sleep.

Roy's talk drew to a close. "I know each one of you gets frustrated sometimes with school, and I don't blame you at all. I've been frustrated myself, but don't try so hard that it makes you angry. Put it away and come back to it. You can figure it out. Keep learning, and you can do anything. You have it made."

Epilogue
Roy's Message

ROY DOESN'T RIDE anymore, but he is still an inspiration to me and to everyone he meets. He attended Winters Community Christian School, learning how to do math and brushing up on his reading and writing, until the school closed its doors in the spring of 2013, when Roy was seventy-four years old. Most days he can be found in Steady Eddy's coffee shop downtown, sipping coffee and socializing with everyone who walks through the door. Mom and Roy still run errands together, after which Roy usually comes out and spends some time at Red Tail Farm.

Roy continued to expand his post-retirement activities in 2013 when he joined the Solano County Sheriff Posse as a volunteer; Mom and I had been recruited during a parade, when the sheriff liaison was impressed by Cassie's stoic acceptance of all the armor both she and I wore. Mom and I rode our horses with the Posse, while Roy joined the contingent of retired men riding in Sheriff Jeeps and Humvees at parades.

In the spring of 2014, I received a call from Jesse, my lifelong friend who had recently received her teaching credential. She was working at the elementary school of the nearby town of Esparto. She got straight to the point. "Some of the kids in my class are being bullied, but they are afraid to tell me who is bullying them. Do you think you could bring Roy to my class to talk to them?"

The next week, Roy and I went to Jesse's classroom, where I witnessed Roy's amazing power of connecting with people. Within minutes of his arrival, the children who were suffering the wrath of bullies poured their hearts out to him; after we left, they finally told Jesse who was bullying them, and she was able to intercede on their behalf and stop the bullies.

A few months later, she invited Roy and me back to her classroom as an end-of-the-year surprise for her students.

The reaction of the students was overwhelming as we stepped into the classroom.

"Roy!"

"Look, it's Roy!"

"Hi, Roy!"

"Wow, Roy's here!"

Jesse hadn't told her students that Roy was coming, but they remembered exactly who he was and welcomed him with sensational enthusiasm. As Roy went around hugging all the students, I slipped out of the classroom to prepare my own surprise for the class.

In the parking lot, Cassie waited in the trailer. My steadfast mare had just weaned her third and final foal. A few years after Racer was born, my lifelong hope of having a horse like the golden Sawdust was finally fulfilled, when Cassie gave birth to Moonlight Delight, a palomino filly that gleams just as beautifully as her grandsire Sawdust. A year later, Shockfire Comet was born, a fiery chestnut colt who is the spitting image of his dam.

The final pregnancy was difficult on Cassie. Partway through, she had a severe case of colic and nearly died. Despite the fact that I weaned Comet early in order to conserve Cassie's strength, she had lost around a hundred pounds by the time she had finished nursing her foal. Afterward, I took special care of my mare in order to ensure her complete recovery: she had as much as she wanted to eat, and I only allowed her to do low-energy activities.

But Cassie has always been an active horse, and she quickly grew bored with her convalescence. Every time the trailer was hitched to the truck, she looked in eager anticipation, hoping that she would be the one chosen to go on a ride. So I compromised, taking her to undemanding activities with the Posse, which included events where her only job was to stand still and allow children to pet her. It was the perfect occupation for the people-loving horse, and the ideal preparation for returning to Jesse's class.

After I texted Jesse to let her know that everything was ready, she and Roy led her class to the parking lot where Cassie and I waited. Once they arrived, Roy introduced the class to one of the animals who had kindled enthusiasm in him since he was young. The children crowded around Cassie and stroked her head, which she had lowered so they could reach. It was a day they would always remember, inspired by a man they would never forget.

Roy left them with a simple message: "You can do anything that you put your mind to. Just keep trying, no matter what anyone tells you. Nobody can stop you."

Acknowledgments

Thank you to the Vacaville Town Square Writers for all your support, encouragement, and feedback while I was finishing this book. Without all of you, this book would've taken twice as long to get published (and would be half as good).